THE PROFESSIONAL HOUSEKEEPER

THE PROFESSIONAL HOUSEKEEPER

Pallab Sengupta
Biswanath Bid

NAMAN PUBLISHER & DISTRIBUTORS
NEW DELHI

Published by
Sangeeta Jain for Naman Publisher & Distributors
7360-B, Prem Nagar,
Gali No.1, Shakti Nagar,
Delhi-110007
PH: 23823642, MOB.: 09013478302
E-mail: rajivjain72@ymail.com

First Published – 2025

ISBN–978-81–920935–9-8

SOLE DISTRIBUTOR
JINDAL BOOK SERVICES
LG-4A, Ganpati Bhawan,
4675-B/21, Ansari Road,
Darya Ganj, Delhi - 110002

Jacket Designed by :
S.M. Graphics

Printed by:
Sachin Printers, Delhi, India

Preface

A characteristic common to all lodging establishments, regardless of size and category, is the need for housekeeping services, which can range from very sophisticated to a simple matter of refreshing rooms once a week. A professional housekeeper is responsible to the domestic bursar. His duties are to make sure all rooms, flats and houses are cleaned and ready for students and that bed linen is available for those who have booked it. He supervises the cleaners to ensure that cleaning the rooms, kitchens, bathrooms, showers and common areas is completed satisfactorily. He is also responsible for checking all rooms after they have been vacated, to agree the return of deposits if no damage has been caused.

With the advent of modern technologies and new markets, the responsibilities of the professional housekeeper is rapidly changing. Now, the professional housekeeper is no longer responsible only for cleaning duties and time schedules, he must be knowledgeable about staff diversity issues, building relations with unions, and maximising the uses of available technology while staying aware of the bottom line. He must also be aware of growing health and safety concerns. This book includes everything from the latest information on cleaning to technological advances in the industry. Students and teachers alike will find this book an invaluable reference tool.

Contents

HERITAGE

LEARNING & DEVELOPMENT CENTER

Heritage Learning and Development Centre (HLDC) is an extended arm of Heritage Institute of Hotel & Tourism (HIHT). Heritage Institute of Hotel & Tourism is an Institute of excellence of the upcoming chain of Management Institutes, founded by D. K. Singh, President. At HIHT, our endeavour is to take education to the higher domains of never ending success. Heritage Institute of Hotel & Tourism provides the best possible infrastructure for pursuing best quality Hotel Management Education. HIHT has three campuses Agra, Shimla and Goa and proposed campuses at Kolkata, Pune, and Singapore.

In the modern era, Hospitality Industry is a reality, fighting for extremely challenging phase and getting into a stability mode. There are SMILES everywhere and this is relatively controlled and guarded, a sign of maturing and learning of Hospitality, which is cyclic in nature. The Hospitality Industry reflects a bright future. Earlier days, hospitality was synonymous with only hotel industry, but today this industry holds its important place with tourism. Hospitality academic in India is still in its nascent stage when compared to the west.

HLDC has been developed through the inputs from the industry and experts from the academics. This panel of experts have gone through the book and made suggestions which were incorporated. Every attempt has been made to thoroughly cover the day to day problems faced in the profession. In this field, as in most any other, it is prudent to remember the old adage, actions speak louder than words. The information given in this book makes the students fit for the industry. It provides about technical skills, personality and soft skills and ability to think and make decision.

This book is designed and presented in an easy to read and easy to understand format. It will be beneficial to both aspiring professionals and those already in the industry.

We hope this text book meets its intended purpose as a practical resource, and serve as a vehicle for promoting the professionalism of this important segment of the Hospitality Industry.

1

The Housekeeping Department

Since the beginning of recorded time, people have travelled and therefore have been in need of lodging. To lodge means to furnish guests with room or quarters, generally on a temporary basis. This broad definition implies that the lodging industry is quite diverse, for the renting of living space can range from a simple room in a boarding house to a spacious suite in a luxury hotel or a bungalow in a lavish resort. Now lodging establishments are an intrinsic part of the hospitality trade and perhaps the most important of the segments into which this industry is divided.

The term 'hotel' derives from the French word *hostel*. The modern French word hotel suggests "a more or less commodious establishment with up-to-date appointments," though this was not necessarily true one hundred years ago. Today, the term hotel defines a lodging establishment offering accommodation, food and beverage, and amenities to guests. Besides hotels, motels and resorts the lodging industry today offers a variety of establishments aimed at fulfilling the needs of the current market. The most common are:

— *Bed and breakfast inns*. These are usually small, privately owned establishments located in suburban and rural locations. They are often uniquely appointed converted private homes that cater to travellers seeking a homey, personal environment.

— *Time-share condominiums.* These are apartments, villas, or bungalows usually built near popular vacation spots that are sold to individual owners who use them or rent them out to transient guests. Time-share owners also have the option of trading with other owners of units located in different parts of the country or the world.

— *Cruise ships.* These can be described as floating luxury hotels/resorts that provide most of the same services and amenities as properties located on land. Having become quite popular in the vacation and convention markets, cruise ships are one of the fastest growing segments of the hospitality industry.

— *Institutional lodging establishments.* Institutional lodging is provided by housing facilities that are integral parts of institutional organizations, such as hospitals, retirement homes, universities, and colleges. In some cases this type of lodging requires limited services, such as weekly cleaning or catered meals, which are provided by contracting companies.

— *Casinos.* These are generally first-class hotels that provide elaborate facilities for gambling, ranging from the ubiquitous slot machine to the sophisticated baccarat or roulette tables. These highly profitable establishments often offer luxurious lodging and lavish entertainment at low cost to attract potential customers. Lodging properties can be independently owned, owned by a multi-unit chain, franchised, or managed by a management company.

Lodging properties that are independently owned are not affiliated with any multiple-property entity and are usually managed by their owners. This type of property still represents the largest segment of the lodging industry. A typical in dependently owned establishment is small in size and is located in a relatively small community. There are advantages and disadvantages to independent operation: on the positive side, independent lodging establishments can provide guests with unique, personalized service while saving royalty and management fees that otherwise would have to be paid to franchisors and/or management companies. On the negative side, such properties may not have name recognition to travellers, they lack collective advertising power, and they are unable to benefit from a national/international reservation system. Often, independently owned and managed properties join reservation referral systems and marketing associations. Chain properties operate under the direct control of the chain's headquarters. Establishments belonging to the same chain display the same logo and offer identical services by category.

When hotel owners lack the operative expertise necessary to manage their properties efficiently, they may choose to contract with a management company. In this case, the owner signs a contract delegating the property's operations to such a company in exchange for either paying a basic fee or allowing the management company to retain an agreed-upon percentage of the revenue or income, or a combination of the two.

Types of Lodging Facilities

Lodging facilities can also be categorized by size. An arbitrary classification can be:

— *Small*: up to 75 rooms

— *Medium*: from 75 to 200 rooms

— *Large*: from 200 to 500 rooms

— *Very large*: more than 500 rooms

The size of a property can be used to estimate the amount of work required of the housekeeping department on a daily basis to maintain the property. Lodging properties can also be categorized by service.

1. *Economy or budget properties* focus on meeting the basic needs of the travelling public-that is, clean, comfortable rooms that are not expensive. The market segments typically attracted to economy properties are guests travelling with children, bus tours, and budget-minded retirees. Many of these properties do not offer food and beverage services except for breakfast, although they all feature TV and some have a swimming pool, whirlpool, and tennis courts.
2. *Mid-market properties* offer all the amenities expected in a "home -away-from -home setting." Restaurants, coffee shops, bars, luggage service, meeting rooms, health club, and room service are generally offered in such properties. The quality of bed linen, towels, room furniture, lobby decor, and customer service must be good or very good. Travellers who frequent properties of this type are business people, individual tourists, conventioneers, and guests wishing to receive a guaranteed level of excellent service.

A characteristic common to all lodging establishments, regardless of size and category, is the need for housekeeping services, which can range from very sophisticated to a simple matter of "refreshing" rooms once a week. For instance, a luxury hotel, casino, or resort usually requires that the rooms be impeccably clean, that the bed linen is changed every time the bed is used, and that turndown service is provided daily. On the other hand, the service for a university residence room might consist in just providing the tenant with a fresh set of sheets every Sonday morning. Mid-range service hotels generally require that guestrooms are thoroughly cleaned daily, that bed and bathroom linen is changed every day, and that 24-hour housekeeping service is provided seven days a week. In any case, because housekeeping services must always be provided, the management of the housekeeping department in every lodging establishment is of critical importance to the success of the property.

It is essential that future graduates of hospitality programs understand the options that the industry offers regarding housekeeping management positions. Graduates wishing to achieve the position of executive housekeeper in a relatively short period of time should keep in mind that a small or medium-sized property does generally offer the best opton for candidates to reach their goal. In large or very large establishments, where housekeeping operations are quite complex, it will take longer for candidates to become managers of the department. In any case, the position of executive housekeeper will always be a challenging and rewarding one as well as an adequate springboard from which to work toward the goal of becoming the property's general manager.

ORGANISATION OF HOUSEKEEPING DEPARTMENT

As one of the most integral departments within the hotel, the Housekeeping Department is responsible for the immaculate care and upkeep of all guest rooms and public spaces. Individuals who excel in our Housekeeping Departments have an eye for detail and a commitment to the training, development and motivation of a diverse group of talented employees. A consistent product has always played a vital role in the incredible success of a hotel. The Housekeeping Department has plays a major role in ensuring this product quality. In a competitive hotel market, it is service and cleanliness that really make an impact on our guests and determine whether they will return.

As one of the largest departments within the Hotel, the Housekeeping Department presents an interesting challenge: how do you motivate, train and develop a diverse group of employees to produce a consistently exceptional product? The Housekeeping Manager has the responsibility for all aspects of the Housekeeping Department, from the hiring of employees to the maintenance of operational expenses at or below budget. Interviewing, training, motivating, ordering, receiving and monitoring product quality all play a large role in the typical day of a Housekeeping Manager.

The internal organization of the housekeeping department follows the same pattern as that of the property as a whole. The chain of command begins with the executive housekeeper and goes on to encompass all employees in the department. Besides the section housekeepers, supervisors, and housepersons needed to clean the guestrooms, and the laundry room workers, the housekeeping department needs additional personnel to service other areas of the property, such as offices, public and back-of the-house sections, and linen room.The employees in the department's work force can be classified into management, fixed, evening, laundry, and guestroom cleaning teams.

The executive housekeeper, housekeeping manager, and laundry manager fall under management. These employees are salaried and are required to work a minimum of 40 hours each week. The housekeeping fixed employees are the janitors and the linen room attendants. These workers are usually hourly employees who are guaranteed 5 days' work regardless of guestroom occupancy. The reason for guaranteeing fixed work is that whether or not the guestrooms have been sold out, lobbies, offices and other front and back-of -the-house public areas must be serviced on a daily basis. The evening team takes over the duties of the department at the end of the morning shift when all regular teams clock off.

The jobs generally assigned to the evening shift are cleaning late checkout and day-rate guestrooms, providing turndown service, counting soiled linen, servicing public and back-of-the-house areas, preparing carts for the morning shift, washing guestroom glasses, and filling out guest requests as the evening progresses. As with the janitors, the evening team is composed of hourly employees who are guaranteed 5 days of work regardless of occupancy. The guestroom cleaning and laundry teams are also composed of hourly employees, but the number of hours they are scheduled to work depends on the number of guestrooms sold daily.

The decision as to where to stay was as it is today, based on where you might find a location providing the best food, overnight protection, and clean facilities. Even though the inns were crude, they were gathering places where you could learn the news of the day, socialise, find out the business of the community, and rest. With the growth of transportation-roadways, river travel, railroads, and air travel-Americans became even more mobile. Inns, hotels, motor hotels, resorts, and the like have kept pace, fallen by the wayside, overbuilt, or refurbished to meet quality demands. Just as the traveller of earlier times had a choice, there is a wide choice for travellers today. We therefore have to consider seriously why one specific hotel or inn might be selected over another. In each of the areas we mentioned-food, clean room, sociable atmosphere, meeting space, and security-there has been a need to remain competitive. Priorities in regard to these need areas, however, have remained in the sphere of an individual property's management philosophy.

Professional housekeeping requires a staff with a sense of pride. Housekeeping staffs must show concern for guests, which will make the guests want to return-the basic ingredient for growth in occupancy and success in the hotel business. A prime responsibility of the executive housekeeper is to develop this concern in the staff; it is just as important as the other functions of cleaning bathrooms, making beds, and making rooms ready for occupancy.

Executive Housekeeper

The executive housekeeper supervises all operations of the entire Housekeeping Department. He/she is responsible for the administrative functioning of the department, room service, overall cleanness of the ship excluding the galley and bars. This position also includes the supervision of the baggage discharge. Fluent English language skills required.

Assistant Chief Housekeeper

The assistant chief housekeeper's responsibilities are: day to day supervision of cleaning and maintenance of housekeeping area, guests baggage handling and distribution, inventory control and control of all housekeeping consumables in his/her assigned area, handling guest's special requests and complaints and reporting them to the chief housekeeper. Fluent English language skills required.

Stateroom (Cabin) Steward

The stateroom (cabin) steward is responsible for keeping clean and neat guests staterooms (cabins). He/she provides personal assistance to guests, takes care of guests personal laundry requests, replenishes supplies such as drinking glasses, ice, stationary, etc. The steward approaches guests in a professional manner with courtesy and politeness. Fluent English language skill is required.

Assistant Stateroom (Cabin) Steward

The assistant stateroom (cabin) steward assists the stateroom steward in cleaning guests staterooms (cabins) and passageways, empting wastebaskets and transports trash, transferring the daily linen to the laundry. The assistant steward must deal with guests in a professional manner with courtesy and politeness. Good English language skill is required.

Bell Man

The bell man assists with room service if needed. He/she transfers guests' luggage to and from the ship at each cruise. An applicant must be able to carry heavy parcels. Fluent English is compulsory.

Cleaner

The cleaner is responsible for cleaning the public area, transporting trash, maintaining a safe and sanitary environment. He/she is responsible for storage of all the cleaning supplies.

Responsibilities of Housekeeping Department

The Housekeeping Department performs a variety of functions. It is usually situated at the laundry room or any other convenient place close to Housekeeping Supplies. The Housekeeping Department is responsible for:

- Neatness and cleanliness of all guest rooms and most public areas
- Maintenance of recycled and non-recycled cleaning inventories

Some of the above mentioned functions might however be leased to a concessionaire. In this case, hotel shall still have a housekeeping department but to a minimum number of staff. The housekeeping department is headed by an executive housekeeper.

The areas of responsibility of the housekeeping department will be different depending on the size of the property. In small lodging operations the executive housekeeper is usually in charge of the cleaning and upkeep of most areas. In this particular case, very close cooperation between housekeeping and other departments is necessary to have the job done efficiently. For instance, if housekeeping is in charge of cleaning the banquet rooms, the manager needs to know the type and time of functions in order to provide the necessary service. In some cases, because the preparation and service of food begins very early in the morning and ends quite late in the evening, the cleaning function in food and beverage areas must be provided late at night. In large properties, the division of work by area is spread out among the different operating departments.

Before contracting out cleaning tasks, it is important to obtain cost estimates from two or three different sources based on the size of the areas and the type and frequency of the cleaning desired. Once the contract has been signed, it is essential to check the quality of the work performed by the contractor. In no case should the cost of the services contracted be substantially higher than the cost of the same services performed by in-house personnel. An ideal division of work in large properties would keep the housekeeping department from having to clean areas that are operated by the food and beverage or engineering divisions. There are several reasons for this: the housekeeping department usually does not have the necessary technical resources, the time, nor the expertise to clean ovens, walk-in refrigerators, kitchen hoods, and swimming pools or to prune palm trees and trim rose bushes. Once the cleaning and maintenance responsibilities for all the areas of the property have been established, the respective department heads must plan the activities necessary for the upkeep of their areas, secure sufficient resources, and provide personnel to service them effectively.

The first step in planning the upkeep of the different areas assigned to the housekeeping department is to establish a list of the items that need to be regularly cleaned and maintained. A cleaning inventory list for guestrooms, for instance, will include all items that need to be cleaned, checked, and maintained in each room. The list should follow the sequence that section housekeepers keep when servicing guestrooms, for example, beginning with the entrance door to the rooms, standing lamps, window sills, furniture, and so on and ending with vacuuming the carpet. Another example of cleaning inventory would be that drawn for the lobby of the hotel, which might include not only furniture and fixtures but a water fountain, plants, bookcase, chandelier and so on. Area cleaning inventories can be combined with cleaning frequency schedules, including what needs to be cleaned and how often the items must be cleaned in one single document.

Once the area cleaning inventory lists have been prepared, the frequency for cleaning and maintenance of each item should be established. Generally items need to be cleaned daily, biweekly, weekly, monthly, and so on. Examples of daily service in the lobby area would be the windowsills; plants could be dusted twice a week, the water fountain polished once a week, the air vents on the wall once a month, and so forth. Besides cleaning items on a regular basis, most areas are deep cleaned once or twice a year. In this case, the cleaning crews scrape and scrub every nook and cranny until all surfaces are spotless.

Deep cleaning projects generally coincide with low occupancy periods and are coordinated with repairs being done in the area by the engineering department. After compiling cleaning inventories and frequency schedules, performance standards must be established. Performance standards are used to inform subordinates of the equipment and supplies they must use to clean an item, of the method or way of doing the job, and of the expected cleaning outcomes. It is not good enough to tell section housekeepers and janitors to "clean well." "Cleaning well may mean different levels of cleanliness to different people. An example of performance standard to clean a vanity top could be: Spray all-purpose cleaner on the vanity top and wipe the surface clean with a sanitized rag, wiping it dry until no spots, marks, or specks remain."

The development of cleaning performance standards should be established keeping in mind the direct input of the workers who are assigned to do the cleaning. The written cleaning standards should be a part of the department's standard operating procedures (SOPs) and strictly observed during the training period of new employees. Properties that have written cleaning standards in place are able to measure employee performance by comparing the worker cleaning outcomes with the established standards.

The assignment of guestrooms for daily cleaning is usually done randomly in small hotels. That is, the section housekeepers and gathered at the beginning of the shift and giver, a number of rooms to service on an individual basis. In large hotels, however, house keeping teams should be formed to which the same sections of rooms are consistently assigned.

There are several advantages to allotting the guestrooms to teams. Individual housekeepers take ownership of the rooms they clean day in and day out, showing pride for the work they perform, which increases their morale. Teams create a sense of unity, of common interests and responsibilities by which room attendants are less likely to let their partners down by calling in sick, thus improving attendance. A team may consist of four or five section housekeepers, a team supervisor, and a houseperson.

The section housekeeper cleans guestrooms while the supervisor coordinates the work of the teams and inspects rooms. The housepersons assist in the work by providing the team with supplies, hauling the trash, vacuuming the hallways, moving heavy objects around, and so on. Guestrooms are divided by creating a pictorial representation of all rooms and allocating a certain number of them to every section housekeeper of each team. The criteria for guestroom cleaning workload vary from hotel to hotel depending on the size of the rooms, the number of furniture and fixture pieces to be cleaned, and the level of quality that management wishes to provide. As the workers need to be given two days off per week to avoid overtime, the department will need a larger number of workers to substitute for those who are off. The problem becomes more complicated if the property operates an on-premise laundry.

Housekeeping functions is no more limited to cleaning rooms; it has gone beyond it. New trends are emerging in the segment and among them is the birth of health-conscious guests who demand, among other things, eco-friendly products of international quality. Personal care products like soaps and other toiletries have moved from being chemical-based to natural and ayurvedic products. There is a growing popularity for eco-friendly products; even the packaging is eco-friendly. Virgin propylene is being used for the packaging and lead-free ink is being used for printing on the packages. Cold-crafted soap is the new product which is picking up in the hospitality market. This soap maintains the glycerine level in the soaps and is more skin-friendly.

Apart from personal care products, hygiene maintenance has seen the evolution of products like soap dispensers, hand-dryers and tissue dispensers. They have been in the market for a long time now, the only development it has seen is the use of sensor-operated dispensers and dryers which run on battery or electricity. These options are the best when it comes to keeping up the sanitation of public washrooms. A product which is closely linked with hygiene and sanitation is the use of tissue papers. Innovation of these products is dependent on the technological advances.

Hotels often outsource their laundry, but a more cost-effective method is using in-house washers and dryers. With the evolution of a single system which washes and dries clothes in the same machine, the washer extractor will definitely add to the cost effectiveness of the hotel. To reduce costs even further, use of disposable products like pillow covers and spa garments made of non-woven fabrics would be an economical option. This will also help maintain hygiene. Technological advances can also be relied upon so as to check unwanted and unchecked use of electronic appliances like television and air-conditioning by the housekeeping staff. The swipe card keys used by the guest and the staff are different and only with the use of the guest's swipe card can the appliances be used.

Upkeep of the look and décor of a property is also the responsibility of the housekeeping department. The look has also changed drastically with a number of companies coming in to provide complete renovation solutions to hotels. Adding to the look of a hotel room is the kind of upholstery used, colours, etc.

Even the linen used has undergone changes. The use of bed strips instead of entire bedcovers is an interesting change; the quality has become more skin friendly. The use of jacquard, where products can have colour prints on them, should also see a growth in the future. Hotels can customise their linen products, giving a greater brand recall. The only hindrance at the moment for these products is its cost of manufacturing.

Functions of Housekeeping Managemer

The elements that today's housekeeping managers work with are ideas, things, and people. These are the main components of an organisation and are in the center of the figure. The manager's task that is related to ideas is to think conceptually about matters that need to be resolved. The task related to things is to administer or manage the details of executive affairs. The task related to people is to exercise leadership and influence people so that they accomplish desired goals. The functions of a manager can be thought of as continuous functions and sequential functions. Many times a question may be asked: "But what does the manager do?" The manager should be seen to do several continuous functions, as well as several sequential functions.

Continuous functions

The continuous functions relating to ideas and conceptual thinking are to *analyse problems.* Those related to things and administration are to *make decisions,* and those related to people and leadership are to *communicate* successfully. Problems are analysed, facts gathered, causes learned, alternative solutions developed, decisions made, conclusions drawn, communications generated, and understanding assured.

Sequential functions

The sequential functions of management are more recognisable as a part of the classical definition of management. They involve the planning, organising, staffing, directing, and controlling of ideas, things, and people. Mackenzie sets forth various activities in each of these sequential functions that should be studied and recalled whenever necessary. A manager's sequential functions are divided into five areas—planning, organising, staffing, directing, and controlling. The management plan involves seven basic activities:

— *Forecasting:* Establishing where present courses will lead

— *Setting objectives:* Determining desired results

— *Developing strategies:* Deciding how and when to achieve goals

— *Programming:* Establishing priorities, sequence, and timing of steps

— *Budgeting:* Allocating resources

— *Setting procedures:* Standardising methods

— *Developing policies:* Making standing decisions on important recurring matters

Getting Organised

Getting organised involves arranging and relating work for the effective accomplishment of an objective. Managers organise by making administrative or operational decisions. The four activities involved in getting organised are as follows:

— *Establishing an organisational structure:* Drawing up an organisational chart

— *Delineating relationships:* Defining liaison lines to facilitate coordination

— *Creating position descriptions:* Defining the scope, relationship, responsibilities, and authority of each member of the organisation

— *Establishing position qualifications:* Defining the qualifications for people in each position

The third sequential function, staffing, involves people. Leadership now comes into play and communication is established to ensure that understanding takes place. There are four activities:

— *Selecting employees:* Recruiting qualified people for each position

— *Orienting employees:* Familiarising new people with their environment

— *Training:* Making people proficient by instruction and practice

— *Developing.* Improving knowledge, attitude, and skills

The first three sequential functions of management—planning, organising, and staffing—might be performed before an operation gets under way. The last two sequential functions—directing and controlling—are carried out after the operation has begun or is in process. As with other managerial relationships involving people, leadership is accomplished through communication. In the directing of operations, there are five basic activities:

— *Delegating:* Assigning responsibility and exacting accountability for results

— *Motivating:* Persuading and inspiring people to take a desired action

— *Coordinating:* Relating efforts in the most efficient combination

— *Managing differences:* Encouraging independent thought and resolving conflict

— *Managing change:* Stimulating creativity and innovation in achieving goals.

The final sequential function of management is to control organisations and activities to ensure the desired progress toward objectives. There are five basic activities in the controlling of operations:

- — *Establishing a reporting system:* Determining what critical data arc needed
- — *Developing performance standards:* Setting conditions that will exist when key duties are well done
- — *Measuring results:* Ascertaining the extent of deviation from goals and standards
- — *Taking corrective action:* Adjusting plans, counselling to attain standards, replanning and repeating the several sequential functions as necessary
- — *Rewarding:* Praising, remunerating, or administering discipline.

Employee Characteristics

The following employee characteristics are commonly found in man in housekeeping departments.

- — Cultural diversity abounds in most housekeeping departments. Racial minorities, particularly black and Hispanic employees, are to be found in numbers that are disproportionate to their representation in the general population.
- — The reason for this situation is obvious; the doors of opportunity have been closed to these Americans for generations. Consequently, these Americans have gravitated to those few areas of employment left open to them.
- — In many parts of the world, English is not the predominant language spoken in the housekeeping department. In fact, in many housekeeping departments many workers can neither speak nor write in English.
- — Housekeeping often attracts individuals with little formal education. Many workers are functionally illiterate, and others can be classified as being "math

illiterate." This can have a particularly telling effect upon departmental efficiency and communications.

— Many of the employees come from lower socioeconomic backgrounds. These environments can often be a major factor in the formation of employee attitudes and behaviours that are not compatible with traditional corporate values.

— A worker may often have emotional or economic problems, or may even have a dependency problem. It is not suggested that the executive housekeeper is the only manager within the hotel who faces these problems, but many would argue that the frequency of these problems is higher in housekeeping than in other areas. Housekeeping often attracts displaced housewives, single parents, and former welfare recipients who have a higher incidence of these problems.

Although there may be numerous properties throughout the world where these traits and characteristics are not found in the employees of the housekeeping department, they do appear frequently enough to require the astute housekeeping manager to prepare for such eventualities. The motivation of employees is accomplished by the manager having created an environment in which employees can motivate themselves. Managers cannot hope to directly motivate other human beings; however, they can provide a climate where self-motivation will take place.

Employee Training

A formal training program is an indispensable element in achieving productivity goals. There are, however, certain training approaches and concerns that are not being addressed by all housekeeping administrators. These concerns include the educational background of the staff. Many housekeeping workers may be illiterate or may not be able to communicate in English. Written training materials, such as manuals, posters, and written tests, are quite useless when the staff cannot read, write, or speak the English language. Special audio/visual training materials are often required in housekeeping departments, and the written training materials must often be made available to the workers in Spanish or other languages. The introduction of these materials does not rectify the problem, however.

Many housekeeping departments have initiated remedial educational programs so that employees can not only learn to read and write in English; but can also earn their high school diplomas.The executive housekeeper does not have to implement these remedial programs from scratch; he or she can turn to a number of sources of assistance found in most communities, such as the public school or the community college system. These sources can often provide qualified bilingual adult instruction at little or no cost to the company. Another tactic is to reimburse employee tuition if remedial classes are completed at the local community college.

The payoff to the housekeeping department is twofold. First, productivity benefits because the level of communication has increased. Second, the esteem level of the employees should certainly increase when they begin to achieve their personal educational goals, and a self-assured workforce will ultimately become a more competent and productive workforce.

Delegation

Delegation is one of five activities of direction. Others view delegation as the most valuable activity. The other activities—motivation, coordination, managing differences, and managing change—can be seen as stemming from a manager's ability to delegate properly. Too often we hear the phrase, "delegation of responsibilities and authority." In fact, it is impossible to delegate a responsibility. To delegate actually means to pass authority to someone who will act in behalf of the delegator. The passing of such authority does not relieve the delegator of the responsibility for action or results, although there is an implied accountability of the person to whom power has been delegated to the person having that power.

The responsibility of a manager for the acts or actions of his or her subordinates is therefore absolute and may not be passed to anyone else. When an executive housekeeper is assigned overall responsibility for directing the activities of a housekeeping department, carrying out this responsibility may require the completion of thousands of tasks, very few of which may actually be performed by the executive housekeeper. It is therefore a responsibility of management to identify these tasks and create responsibilities for subordinates to carry them out.

A good operational definition of delegation is the creation of a responsibility for, or the assignment of a task to, a subordinate, providing that person with the necessary authority (power) to carry out the task and exacting an accountability for the results of the subordinate's efforts. The lack of any one of the three elements of this definition creates a situation whereby the manager abdicates the responsibility to manage. Thorough and complete delegation, where possible, will free the manager from tasks that can be performed by subordinates, allowing the manager time to manage the operation.

Realationship with Other Departments

The Executive Housekeeper is the head of housekeeping

and is therefore directly responsible for managing what is in most cases the largest department of the establishment. The position of executive housekeeper in the organizational chart is that of department head, equal in rank to the front office manager, the security manager, and the remaining managers in charge of departments in other divisions. In smaller properties, the division directors do not exist; instead, department heads manage the different units and report directly to the general manager. The housekeeping department is an integral part of all the areas into which a lodging operation is divided.

Although housekeeping's primary communication takes place with the front office and engineering departments, a strong relationship must exist with an the other units of the property as well. For instance, room service, a department in the food and beverage division that delivers food to guestrooms, must be in direct contact with housekeeping for the removal of trays and carts. The sales department, which often must have access to ready rooms to be shown to meeting planners or tour operator representatives, must communicate this need to the housekeeping department.

Relationship with Front Office

Guestrooms in hotels are sold by the front office. The front desk must know at every given moment what rooms have been cleaned and are available for occupancy. Housekeeping must provide the front desk with a listing of rooms that are ready for occupancy so guests can be checked in. If the communication between the two departments is poor or breaks down, delays in guest checking will occur or people will be checked into rooms that are thought to be ready but that in fact are occupied or not ready. If this happens often, the property's reputation will suffer. The cycle of communication begins early each day, when the front desk provides the housekeeping department with a written report called the night clerk's room report.

The housekeeping employee in charge of opening the house transfers the information received from the front desk into forms to be distributed to the housekeeping supervisors who, in turn, will notify the room attendants before they begin to work in their respective sections. As guests check in and out of the hotel throughout the day, the front desk notifies housekeeping. When discrepancies are found between the status of rooms received from the night clerk and the physical inspection of the rooms, the front desk is immediately notified. For instance, if the front desk reports that a certain room is vacant and housekeeping finds it occupied, a discrepancy exists and the front desk should be notified. There are several reasons why discrepancies may occur. The most common are:

— A guest switches from one room to another and the front desk neglects to change its records.

— An error is made by the night clerk when filling out the night clerk's report.

— A guest is given the wrong room key by mistake.

— The room is used by an unauthorized employee.

— The room is sold by the front desk without being recorded, and the money is pocketed by the clerk.

— A guest checks in or out between the time the report is made and the check is conducted.

The communication between the housekeeping department and the front desk is greatly improved when the property uses a computerized system. For instance, when a guest checks out, the front desk clerk enters the departure in the computer and it appears instantly in the housekeeping monitor. When housekeeping has rooms ready to be sold, the information is entered in the system and it too shows up quickly in the front desk terminal.

Cleaning and inspcction

The room status for each room determines how much effort, time, labor, and hence scheduled staff is needed by the housekeeping department on any shift. The housekeeping department shall first clean rooms for expected arrivals first, then stayover rooms and eventually vacant rooms.The reason is that rooms for new arrivals takes more time to be cleaned to hotel standards again and that guests might come any time to request their rooms even before the pre-determined beginning of check-in time. That's why; the housekeeping department shall be communicated from the reservation department on a daily basis expected arrival, stayover, and departure lists to be able to schedule the optimum number of room maids and inspectors for the expected business volume. Moreover, cleaning procedure of guest rooms, there should be a communication between the front office department and housekeeping department to be able to communicate the recent room status of each room. This communication is vital because nobody would like to make a guest wait in the lobby because his/her room is not yet clean or due to the fact that the housekeeping department did not communicate on real time the status to the front office. Lastly, the housekeeping department shall ensure that every room maid shall use efficiently most of his valuable time in cleaning not in going back and forth in the corridors. Yet, since some hotels might operate under the manual or Semi-automated systems, some delays and hence, problems might occur. To illustrate, let's consider the guest room cleaning process along with the different operating modes under which a hotel might operate:

Manual system

Under this system, due to the fact that room maids shall first clean rooms for new arrival, then stayover rooms and at last vacant rooms, these very cleaning personnel have two ways to do it:

— Post to cleaning each room, go to the housekeeping department, inform them about the status and then come back to clean the next room. This would solve the potential problem that a guest might be waiting for a clean room due to a communication of the housekeeping department not in real tome. However this would decrease the number of rooms cleaned and inspected by room maids and inspectors, which would mean higher housekeeping labor costs.

— Post to cleaning certain category of rooms, and/or all rooms, room maids inform the housekeeping department, and then inspectors would inspect all rooms, at the same time, inform the department about the recent statuses. This would increase maids' and inspectors' efficiency but would cause guests waiting in the lobby to be escorted to their rooms.

Semi-automated system

Under this system, room maids and inspectors might use either a phone machine situated at the center of each corridor, or pagers and beepers to communicate the recent room status. This proved to be efficient as to minimize labor cost and the time that a guest spends on the lobby waiting to be escorted to his/her room. However, this might create some problems:

— Upon the usage of beepers, the housekeeping department doesn't know exactly which room is cleaned or inspected, therefore will spend needless time to be certain which would put more stress on check-in personnel to convince a waiting guest in the lobby area.

— Guests tend to be both not at ease and dissatisfied seeing hotel personnel in their rooms using beepers and might think that something wrong happened in their rooms.

Fully automated system

This is the best system, which eliminates nearly all time losses spent by room maids and inspectors, to inform the housekeeping department and the time needed to be spent needlessly at the lobby area. Under this very system, each room maid and inspector, prior to the fulfillment of his or her duties in the room, can send a coded message from the guest's room telephone to the housekeeping department. Later an electronic message can be send automatically to check-in personnel confirming that the room is cleaned to standards and waiting for the next arrival.

Room status report

The front office and the housekeeping department shall prepare at the same time, as frequent as needed by management, their room status reports, which lists, according to each department, the recent room status of each room in the hotel. Later, these two reports shall be cross-referenced and compared to detect room status discrepancies and correct them as soon as possible in order to maximize room revenue, detect skippers before it is too late. In the manual system, room status reports shall be reconciled at least each hour. This very frequency might increase as the business volume increases. In the semi-automated system, reconciliation shall be at least once per shift. Lastly under the fully automated system, since housekeeping and front office department's communication is ensured electronically on real time, reconciliation needs to be done only at the night shift by the night auditor. If at the reservation or registration process, guests have communicated certain specific needs related to certain specific amenities and/or facilities that needed to be provided in the room, then the front office department shall communicate this directly to the Housekeeping department or indirectly to the concierge who shall further communicate this to the housekeeping department and follow up to ensure the actual provision in a timely and accurate manner.

Relation with Maintenance Department

The relationship between housekeeping and the maintenance department must be as close as that with the front office. Every piece of equipment, fixtures, and furniture in the guestrooms, hallways, linen and laundry rooms, public areas, and employee locker rooms must be in perfect working order at all times. The number of items that may be in need of repairs in a single guestroom can be substantial: beds, chairs, desks, TVs, radios, lights, doors, toilets, faucets, walls, heating, air conditioning, and so on. It is therefore imperative that good communication between the two departments exists at all times. For instance, if a guestroom lock is broken, maintenance must be notified, the room must be put out of order, the work performed, the area cleaned, and the room put back in vacant ready status.

There are two types of maintenance performed by the engineering department in hospitality properties. Regular maintenance is performed when an item is broken and needs to be repaired. In this case, a three-part work order form is filled out by a housekeeping employee who forwards two copies to engineering and keeps the duplicate filed until the work is completed. When work is completed, one of the copies is returned to housekeeping for comparison, the work is inspected, and the area cleaned. When a problem is urgent and engineering does not promptly address it, housekeeping generates a second request work order to remind that department that the work must be completed. If the repair needs to be done in order to be able to sell the room that day, an urgent request is sent to engineering so that the work is given priority over other nonessential jobs.

The orderly flow of information between housekeeping and engineering about items or areas in need of attention is of critical importance. As the housekeeping department staff is directly involved in cleaning most sections of the property, they are in the best position to find areas in need of maintenance or repair. Preventive maintenance consists of inspecting guestrooms and other areas on a regular basis to identify repair and maintenance needs. In most hotels, the executive housekeeper and the chief engineer cooperate in combining room cleaning with preventive maintenance programs. This involves conducting a thorough maintenance inspection of all rooms in the property two or three times a year.

Relation with human resources Department

Communication between the housekeeping and human resources departments is necessary when considering personnel staffing. When an employee is needed in the housekeeping department, an employee requisition is filled out and sent to human resources to initiate the process. After receiving the request, human resources advertises for the position, pre-screens the candidates, conducts the first interview, and checks references. The final candidates are then sent to housekeeping for a second interview and hiring selection. Human resources is usually also involved in the orientation of new housekeeping employees, at which time the company's philosophy, compensation package, pay schedule, and rules and regulations are explained in detail to the new worker. This department also ensures that the new employee fills out all necessary forms related to legal residency, income tax, and personal information. Good communication with human resources will result in hiring the right employees to fill housekeeping vacancies.

Relation with Food Service Department

Food and beverage is the second major revenue center in the property after the rooms division. The food and beverage division in large hotels comprises the property's kitchens, restaurants, coffee shops, cafeterias, bars, lounges, banquets, catering services, clubs, and room service. In large hotels, the housekeeping department should only be indirectly involved in the cleaning of food and beverage outlets. However, the communication between food and beverage and housekeeping is necessary in some specific areas. There must be good cooperation regarding the pickup of room service material from guestroom areas. Housekeeping must see to it that hallways are free from trays and carts placed there by guests and section housekeepers; therefore, calls to room service must be regularly placed to remind this department to clear all areas.

The laundry room must provide the food and beverage department with clean napery on a daily basis. This often means that the laundry manager must request that the soiled linen be delivered to the laundry room on time, properly sorted out, and free from food scraps and table debris. Furnishing clean uniforms to cooks, waiters, and bartenders is also usually the responsibility of the housekeeping department. As communication with food and beverage service personnel is traditionally difficult, efforts must be made to establish good relationships between departments.

Relation with Sales Department

The primary goal of the sales and marketing division is to sell the products and services offered by the property. Given that cleanliness is one of the most important reasons for guests to choose a particular lodging property, the onus of providing this critical service falls on the housekeeping department. There must be good communication between sales and housekeeping if customer satisfaction is to be achieved. For instance, if sales and marketing has guaranteed late check-out to a large group of guests attending a convention without notifying housekeeping, some of the rooms might not be cleaned in time to be available for a tour group scheduled to check-in that same evening. If sales and marketing has promised that forty rooms will be available for early check-in to a company attending a conference at the property and housekeeping has not been notified, there might not be enough manpower that morning to clean the rooms on time. Communication between sales and housekeeping is also necessary when specific rooms or suites must be available for inspection to meeting planners who are considering the property for a possible convention.

2

Responsibilities of Professional Housekeeper

A professional housekeeper is responsible to the domestic bursar. His/her duties are to make sure all rooms, flats and houses are cleaned and ready for students and that bed linen is available for those who have booked it. Also he/she supervises the cleaners to ensure that cleaning the rooms, kitchens, bathrooms, showers and common areas is completed satisfactorily. The professional housekeeper is responsible for checking all rooms, flats and houses after they have been vacated, to agree the return of deposits if no damage has been caused. He/she is available to anyone who may have a problem with any aspect of cleaning.

A professional housekeeper's primary job responsibility is to maintain the employer's home in a clean and presentable manner at all times. A professional housekeeper may live in or live out, and may be employed on either a full time or a part time basis. A professional housekeeper is 'hands on' in the performance of his/her job responsibilities. A professional housekeeper may supervise other household staff, but this is not the norm. A professional housekeeper may be assisted in the performance of his/her duties by a maid.

A professional housekeeper's duties may include any of the following:

- — Cleaning the interior of the home and the immediate areas outside (patios, porches, decks, walks)
- — Kitchen maintenance - dishes, cupboards, pantry, counters and floors.
- — Laundry (clothing and household linens)
- — Bed making, routine bedding and linen changes
- — Meal preparation and service
- — Assisting with the cooking and serving for special events
- — Grocery shopping and other household errands
- — Keeping the household supplies fully stocked
- — Receive & serve guests
- — Pet care
- — Plant care (household)
- — Silver Polishing
- — Secure/supervise tradesmen/contracors
- — Organization: may rotate seasonal clothing in closets, maintain pantry and routinely clear out of date and spoiled items.
- — House-sitting while the employer is out of town
- — Occasional childcare
- — Household bookkeeping and/or accounting tasks

The position of professional housekeeper does not require special education. Skills required include self starter, time management, organization, tact, honesty, and basic money handling and accounting. May be a uniformed staff position. May require dietary training if meal planning is required. Professional housekeeper is supervised by the homeowner in smaller households, and by the Household Manager in larger households and estates.

HISTORY OF HOUSEKEEPING

A professional housekeeper or servant is one who works, and often also lives, within the employer's household. Servants are distinguishable from serfs or slaves in that they are compensated, that is, they must receive payment for their work. They are also free to leave their employment at any time, although socio-economic conditions and laws relating to working in a foreign country may make that difficult. In large households, there can be a large number of professional housekeepers doing different jobs, often as part of an elaborate hierarchy.

A butler is a senior housekeeper, whose duties traditionally included handling the wines of the household and some management of the other servants. Female housekeepers are often called maids. Housekeepers perform typical housekeeping chores such as cooking, ironing, washing, cleaning the house, buying foods and drinks, accompanying the female head of the household for grocery shopping, taking the family dog for a walk, and taking care of the children. On many places in some countries, maids replace the role of a nurse in taking care of the elderly and people with disabilities. Maids often are expected to work at least fifteen hours per day.

Pre-Modern Age

Housekeeping service, or the employment of people for wages in their employer's residance, is also sometimes simply called "service". It evolved into a hierarchical system in various countries at various times. Prior to the labour reforms of the 20th century, servants had no protection in law. The only real advantage that service provided was the provision of meals and accommodation in addition to the modest wage. Also, service was an apprentice system; there was room for advancement through the ranks. However, it was also perilous, particularly for females, as there was no protection from unscrupulous employers or members of the family. In Britain this system peaked towards the close of the Victorian Era, perhaps reaching its most complicated and rigidly structured state during the Edwardian period, which reflected the limited social mobility of the time. Today organisations such as Kalayaan support the growing number of migrant housekeepers.

Modern Age

Housekeeping service reached its height during the Edwardian and Victorian ages in Great Britain and the Gilded Age in the United States. The emancipation of middle-class women in the late 20th century and their entry into the professional workforce meant that middle-class households were deprived of an important source of unpaid housekeeping labour. This has given rise to a sharp increase in the employment of cleaners and nannies. That said, the number of households employing full-time housekeeping service has reduced greatly.

In other places, such as Latin America, India, Africa and mainland China, most housekeepers are from the same country in which they work. They may commute from home though they are usually "live-in" domestics, meaning they receive room and board as part of their salaries, sometimes they only receive room and board. All these countries have very large differences in the income of urban and rural households, and between different socio-economic classes.

In Brazil, housekeepers must be hired under a registered contract and have most of the rights of any other workers, which includes a minimum wage, limited working hours, remunerated vacancies and a remunerated day-off per week. It is not uncommon, however, to hire servants without registering them. Since servants come almost always from the lower, uneducated classes, they are sometimes ignorant of their rights, especially in the rural zone. Nevertheless, it is not unusual that domestics employed without a proper contract sue their employers to get compensation from abuses.

Although there are some from mainland China who work in the United States and Europe as housekeeping staff, the vast majority of housekeepers in mainland China are from China's rural areas who are employed by urban families. Because of the large gap between urban and rural incomes, and the lack of employment opportunities in the countryside, even an ordinary middle class urban family can afford to employ a full time live-in servant.

Many countries and some industries, such as cruise lines, import housekeepers from abroad, usually poorer countries, through recruitment agencies and brokers because their own nationals are no longer obliged or inclined to work in underpaid, difficult or exploitive jobs. This includes most Middle Eastern countries, Hong Kong, Singapore, Malaysia and Taiwan. For most of these countries, the number of housekeepers run into the hundreds of thousands. There are at least one million housekeepers in Saudi Arabia.

For various reasons, many employers require their housekeepers to wear a 'uniform' or other "housekeepers clothes" when being in their employers home. This is seldom the case in places such as Taiwan, Singapore, and Hong Kong where small middle-class families usually hire only one worker. The uniform is usually simple, and was even back in the 19th century and 20th century. Female servants would wear long, plain, dark-coloured dresses or a black skirt with white belt and a white blouse or shirt and black shoes, and male servants and butlers would wear something from a simple suit, down to a white shirt, often with tie, and knickers.

Maid Service

Maid service, also known as a cleaning service, is a business which provides cleaning services as a convenience to homeowners who do not have the time to clean their own homes. Maid services have become increasingly common in many developed cultures, partly because of the rise in two-income families.

A housemaide making-bed

A maid service may be more expensive than simply hiring a part-time maid, but it offers a number of advantages. Usually the service will provide not only someone to do the cleaning, but also all of the necessary cleaning supplies. Also, as a bona fide employer, the service is responsible for withholding Social Security and other income taxes. Third, a service is insured and often bonded, so it can be held accountable if something is stolen or missing.

Maid services are becoming more popular in cities in particular; perhaps a sign of a relatively well-off population. Historically and traditionally, cleaning was considered a woman's role, but as more and more women have joined the workforce, the time pressure on families with children has grown, so paying a service for cleaning makes sense to persons who can afford it. Additionally, many modern homeowners lack the proper knowledge to use the safest and most effective cleaning products. A cleaning service is a relatively easy sort of business to start, because one needs little more than a phone and one or two workers to get started.

Qualities of a Good Professional housekeeper

Cleanliness, punctuality, order, and method, are essentials in the character of a good professional housekeeper. Without the first, no household can be said to be well managed. The second is equally all-important; for those who are under the housekeeper will take their "cue" from her; and in the same proportion as punctuality governs her movements, so will it theirs. Order is indispensable; for by it we wish to be understood that "there should be a place for everything, and everything in its place." Method, too, is most necessary; for when the work is properly contrived, and each part arranged in regular succession, it will be done more quickly and more effectually.

The professional housekeeper must consider herself as the immediate representative of her mistress, and bring, to the management of the household, all those qualities of honesty, industry, and vigilance, in the same degree as if she were at the head of her own family. Constantly on the watch to detect any wrong-doing on the part of any of the domestics, she will overlook all that goes on in the house, and will see that every department is thoroughly attended to, and that the servants are comfortable, at the same time that their various duties are properly performed. A necessary qualification for a professional housekeeper is, that she should thoroughly understand accounts. She will have to write in her books an accurate registry of all sums paid for any and every purpose, all the current expenses of the house, tradesmen's bills, and other extraneous matter. A housekeeper's accounts should be periodically balanced, and examined by the head of the house. Nothing tends more to the satisfaction of both employer and employed, than this arrangement. It will be found an excellent plan to take an account of every article which comes into the house connected with housekeeping, and is not paid for at the time. The book containing these entries can then be compared with the bills sent in by the various tradesmen, so that any discrepancy can be inquired into and set right. An intelligent housekeeper will, by this means, too, be better able to judge of the average consumption of each article by the household; and if that quantity be, at any time, exceeded, the cause may be discovered and rectified, if it proceed from waste or carelessness.

Although in the department of the cook, the professional housekeeper does not generally much interfere, yet it is necessary that she should possess a good knowledge of the culinary art, as, in many instances, it may be requisite for her to take the superintendence of the kitchen. As a rule, it may be stated, that the housekeeper, in those establishments where there is no house steward or man cook, undertakes the preparation of the confectionary, attends to the preserving and pickling of fruits and vegetables; and, in a general way, to the more difficult branches of the art of cookery. Much of these arrangements will depend, however, on the qualifications of the cook; for instance, if she be an able artiste, there will be but little necessity for the housekeeper to interfere, except in the already noticed articles of confectionary, etc.

Role of Executive Housekeepers

Executive housekeepers direct and control the operations

of housekeeping departments within hotels, hospitals and other establishments. Executive housekeepers inspect rooms for cleanliness and check on other housekeeping tasks to make sure that workers are following proper procedures. They make sure that the work of the housekeeping department falls within the established standards of quality for the hotel. In some establishments executive housekeepers supervise the staff who set up rooms for conventions, banquets, exhibits, and other programmes. Executive housekeepers may be in charge of ordering housekeeping supplies and equipment. They may help in the selection and purchase of new furniture.

Some executive housekeepers work with interior decorators to develop new decorating schemes for rooms and public areas. The housekeeping staff tells the executive housekeeper about damage and equipment that needs repair. Executive housekeepers conduct their own inspections and make recommendations on the relocation of equipment and the use of space. They also develop procedures on how to inform the engineering/ maintenance department when its services are needed. They keep records on personnel, payroll, expenses, and housekeeping activities. They keep management informed about repair work, improvements, personnel difficulties, and expenditures. They submit a yearly budget for review and approval.

In small or medium-sized hotels and motels executive housekeepers may share cleaning chores with the staff. Executive housekeepers who work in small institutions may also be in charge of other operations such as maintenance and ordering food. Housekeepers in hospitals make sure that patients have safe, clean rooms. They follow strict procedures for cleanliness and sanitation to prevent the spread of infection and disease. They develop education programmes for the staff and teach them how to handle contaminated wastes safely. They teach them safety techniques and the correct way to use supplies and equipment.

Executive housekeepers work in clean, attractive, comfortable buildings. Although they usually have their own office, they spend a good part of their time in other parts of the establishment. They may be on their feet most of the day. Housekeepers in resort hotels or motels may work longer hours during the tourist season. Executive housekeepers who live in the hotel have regular hours, but they may be on call at any time. Executive housekeepers in hospitals, schools, and other institutions usually work forty hours a week. Salaries depend on the experience and education of the housekeeper and the size and location of the establishment that employs them.

Some hotels may offer executive housekeepers and their families room and board and use of hotel services. Other benefits are paid vacations, sick leave, hospital insurance, and tuition assistance for continuing education. At one time the job of executive housekeeper went to the person in the housekeeping department with the most experience or seniority. Today, many executive housekeepers have a college degree or have taken advanced courses in business and management. They will have better employment opportunities if they have at least a two-year college degree or have taken some advanced courses in hospitality. They should have a basic knowledge of accounting to keep records and to prepare budgets and reports.

Risks Faced by Housekeepers

Housekeeping in a hotel is a very physically demanding job that includes many, varied tasks. A housekeeper carries out the following tasks:

— making beds

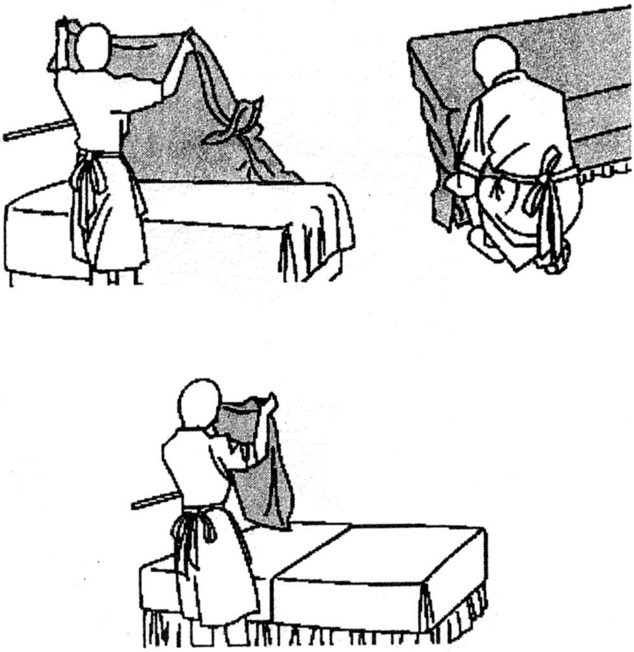

Bed making

— tidying rooms,

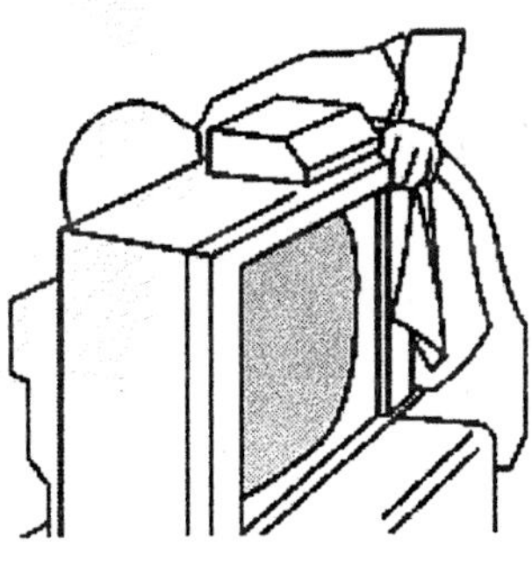

tidying rooms

— cleaning and polishing toilets, taps, sinks, bathtubs and mirrors,

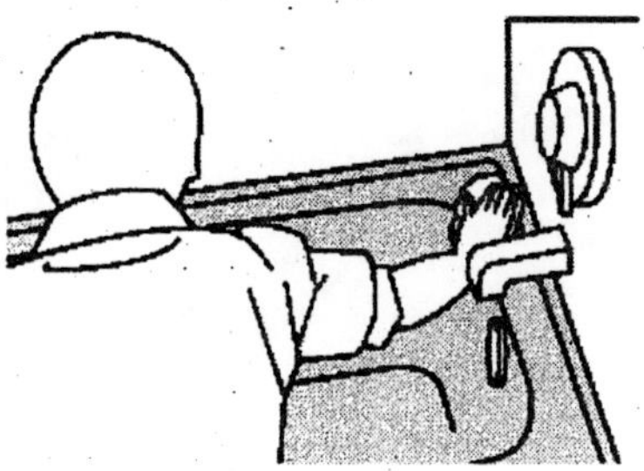

Cleaning

— washing floors,

washing floors

— loundry work, and

A female hosuekeeper doing loundry

— vacuuming.

Vacuuming

The main risk factors for repetitive motion injuries (RMIs) in housekeeping are:

— heavy physical workload and excessive bodily motions which are a high risk for back injuries and

— forceful upper limb motions in awkward positions which are a high risk for neck or shoulder and arm injuries.

Space limitations require workers to use many uncomfortable postures. These are:

— standing or walking,

— stooping,
— squatting,
— kneeling,
— stretching,
— reaching,
— bending,
— twisting, and
— crouching.

A housekeeper changes body position every three seconds while cleaning a room. If we assume that the average cleaning time for each room is twenty-five minutes, we can estimate that a housekeeper assumes 8,000 different body postures every shift. In addition, forceful movements while using awkward body positions include lifting mattresses, cleaning tiles, and vacuuming every shift. Housekeeping is a physically demanding and very tiring job. It can be classified as "moderately heavy" to "heavy" work because the energy required is approximately 4 kilocalories per minute (4 kcal/min.)

Hotel housekeepers work in a unique place. Hotels are usually designed for the comfort of their guests rather than their housekeeping staff. This fact makes it very difficult to improve working conditions for housekeepers by means of better engineering. However, some improvements can be made by selecting more appropriate equipment.

Lighter vacuum cleaners, and lighter service carts with wheels designed for carpeted floors would ease the workload for their operators providing this equipment is always kept in good repair. When new vacuum cleaners are purchased, low noise emissions should be one of the criteria. Improving the body postures that pose a major risk for musculoskeletal disorders seems an unachievable task. Again, this fact results from the peculiarity of hotels as a workplace. To attract guests and remain competitive, hotel management pursues a policy that everything should be "so clean it sparkles". Floors, walls, windows, mirrors, and bathroom fixtures might be adequately cleaned with some form of an extension tool to reduce bending and over-stretching. However, the demand for spotless cleanliness and hygiene, management often requires their cleaning staff to spend extra time and effort cleaning by kneeling, leaning, squatting, crouching, slouching and stretching. These postures will in time contribute to new musculoskeletal injuries and aggravate old ones.

New approaches, other than strictly ergonomic ones, need to be investigated. For example, action can be taken from the administrative level. Options for improvement include:

— job rotation,

— job enrichment and job enlargement,

— team work, and

— education and training on work practices.

Job Rotation

Job rotation is one possible approach. It requires workers to move between different tasks, at fixed or irregular periods. However, it must be a rotation where workers do something completely different. Different tasks must use different muscle groups to allow muscles already stressed to recover.

Job Enlargement

Another approach is job enlargement. This increases the variety of tasks built into the job. It breaks the monotony of the job and avoids overloading one part of the body. Job enrichment involves more autonomy and control for the worker.

Team Work

Team work can provide greater variety and more evenly distributed muscular work. The whole team is involved in the planning of the work. Each team member carries out a set of operations to complete the whole product, allowing the worker to alternate between tasks. This reduces the risk of RMI.

Improving Work Practices

A well-designed job, supported by a well-designed workplace and proper tools, allows the worker to avoid unnecessary motion of the neck, shoulders and upper limbs. However, the actual performance of the tasks depends on individuals. Training should be provided for workers who are involved with housekeeping activities. It is important that housekeeping staff be informed about hazards in the workplace, including the risk of injuries to the musculoskeletal system. Therefore, identification of the hazards for such injury at any given hotel is fundamental.

Individual work practices, including lifting habits, are shaped by proper training. Training should encourage employers and workers to adopt methods that reduce fatigue. For example, it is advisable to plan one's workload and do the heavier tasks at the beginning of the workshift, rather than at the end, when fatigue is at its maximum. When a person is tired, the risk of injuring a muscle is higher. Training should also explain the health hazards of improper lifting and give recommendations on what a worker can do to improve lifting positions. Training should also emphasize the importance of rest periods for the workers' health and explain how active rest can do more for keeping workers healthy than passive rest. The effect of such training can reach far beyond occupational situations because the workers can apply this knowledge also in their off-job lives.

3

Effective Staff Selection

The housekeeping department has the greatest proportion of staffing hours to cover, the most staff, the most hours to cover and it is a cost center. Unlike the restaurant and bar, which are revenue centers, and as long as they are not overstaffed, the more staff you have the more revenue is generated. The housekeeping department is also the one the customers notice most if anything is wrong. You have to have the right number of staff on duty, or it shows.

The housekeeping department can have the following staff depending on the size of hotel.

— Housekeeper and assistant housekeepers,
— room maids,
— cleaners,
— staffmaids,
— cloakroom attendants,
— houseporters,
— valets,
— laundry and linen keeper.

The staff hours of cover depend on the hotel and type of customer, business people require different time schedules to people on holiday with children. The staff need to be scheduled accordingly and in a ratio to the number of guests staying in the hotel. Fortunately, most people book ahead and the workload is known well in advance, especially during peak periods.

The staffing requirement will depend on the occupancy of your hotel. It is possible to get quite good estimates of staff numbers based on average times to do tasks, such as cleaning a room. Then you can allocate 10, or 15, or even 20 rooms to each room maid. It is also quite easy to estimate the total number of staff needed in a year for a task. .

For example, cleaning an occupied room takes 30mins/day, en-suite bathroom 6mins/day, therefore a maid for every 13 occupied rooms. A hotel with 100 rooms (all occupied) needs 8 maids. Then we can sum this up for a year of 365 days, which comes to 2900 maid days per year. We can then divide this by the number of days a maid works per year, say 240, and arrive at a figure of 12 full time maids. Hence we can recruit the 12 maids and start using them on the rooms. We haven't allowed for average occupancy, sickness rates, and a lot of other things which readily come to mind, because at this point, the difficult thing is to find a way of sharing the yearly workload on a day by day basis. This is the difficult part, just how do you allocate the maids so that you have just the right number on every day. Well, the answer depends on where you are at the moment. An existing hotel staffed, is different to a new hotel unstaffed.

Workforce Planning

In its simplest terms workforce planning is getting "the right number of people with the right skills, experiences, and competencies in the right jobs at the right time." This shorthand definition covers a comprehensive process that provides managers with a framework for making staffing decisions based on an organization's mission, strategic plan, budgetary resources, and a set of desired workforce competencies.

Many organizations, both public and private, have developed models for workforce planning. Putting aside variations in terminology, the processes are all very much alike. All rely on an analysis of present workforce competencies; an identification of competencies needed in the future; a comparison of the present workforce to future needs to identify competency gaps and surpluses; the preparation of plans for building the workforce needed in the future; and an evaluation process to assure that the workforce competency model remains valid and that objectives are being met. This process is simple in outline but depends on rigorous and comprehensive analysis of the organization's work, workforce, and strategic direction.

Housekeeping workforce planning requires strong management leadership; clearly articulated vision, mission, and strategic objectives; and cooperative supportive efforts of staff in several functional areas. Strategic planning (GPRA), budget, and human resources are key players in workforce planning. Human resources provides tools for identifying competencies needed in the workforce and for recruiting, developing, training, retraining, or placing employees to build the workforce of the future.

The "why" of housekeeping workforce planning is grounded in the benefits to executive housekeeper. Workforce planning provides them with a strategic basis for making human resource decisions. It allows them to anticipate change rather than being surprised by events, as well as providing strategic methods for addressing present and anticipated workforce issues.

Some components of workforce planning, such as workforce demographics, retirement projections, and succession planning, are familiar to executive housekeepers. Workforce planning provides focus to these components, providing more refined information on changes to be anticipated, the competencies that retirements and other uncontrollable actions will take from the workforce, and key positions that may need to be filled. This in turn allows managers to plan replacements and changes in workforce competencies.

Organizational success depends on having the right employees with the right competencies at the right time. Workforce planning provides executive housekeeperthe means of identifying the competencies needed in the workforce · not only in the present but also in the future and then selecting and developing that workforce.

Housekeeping workforce planning allows organizations to address systematically issues that are driving workforce change. One such issue is age and growing retirement eligibility. In less clear-cut but equally effective ways workforce planning provides executive housekeeperwith tools to address changes in program direction that impact the type of work being performed and allows them to identify ways in which technology may change competencies required in the workforce.

To be useful, a workforce plan must reflect the management and environment of the organization for which it is developed. For that reason, there is no prescribed format for a workforce plan. Instead, the workforce planning process focuses on the basic information needed for the planning process and on the outputs of the process.

A workforce plan must document the workforce analysis, competency assessments, gap analysis, and workforce transition planning that makes up the planning process. These data provide the documentation of the inputs and comprise the basic output of the planning. This information establishes the validity of any workforce plan by demonstrating the links between workforce planning and program management, budget justifications, and human resources work planning.

The primary beneficiary of housekeeping workforce planning is executive housekeeper. Workforce planning provides them with a strategic basis for human resource management decision-making that is based on achieving program goals. Forecasting models based on analysis of the workforce allow them to anticipate turnover and to plan recruiting and employee development to move toward the workforce needed in the future. Knowing the competencies in the workforce and knowing the competencies that will be needed provides managers the information needed to make strategic decisions.

Hiring Employees

Staffing for housekeeping operations involves the activities of selecting, interviewing, orienting, training, and developing personnel to carry out specific functions in the organization for which they are hired. Each activity should be performed with consistency, dispatch, and individual concern for each employee brought into the organization.

Job Specifications

Job specifications are the documents that indicate qualifications, characteristics, and abilities inherently needed in applicants. Job specifications should be written as job descriptions are prepared. Job specifications are simple statements of what the various incumbents to positions will be expected to do. An example of a job specification for a section housekeeper is as follows:

Employee Requisition

Once job specifications have been developed for every position, employee requisitions are prepared for first hirings. Figure 1 is an example of an Employee Requisition.

Employee Requisition

Requisition__________
Department__________

Date__________
Position__________________________
(Number and Title)
New Replacement Number required__________
Classification__________________________
(Full-time, Part-time, Temporary)
Working Hours__________________________
Estimated no. of hours/week__________________
Desired starting date______________________
Starting rate of pay______________________
Base rate__________________________
Specification __________________________
____
____
____
____
____
Special qualifications______________________
____
____
____

____
________Department Manager

Figure 1. Employee requisition

Note the designation as to whether the requisition is for a new or a replacement position and the number of employees required for a specific requisition number. The human resources department will advertise, take applications, and screen to fill each requisition by number until all positions are filled. For example, the first requisition for GRAs may be for 20 GRAs. The human resources department will continue to advertise for, take applications, and screen employees for the housekeeping department and will provide candidates for interview by department managers until 20 GRAs are hired. Should any be hired and require replacing, a new employee requisition will be required.

Sources of Employees

Surveys among hotels or hospitals in your area will indicate the best source for various classifications of employees. Advertising campaigns that will reach these employees are the best method of locating suitable people. Major classified ads associated with mass hirings will specify the need for food service personnel, front desk clerks, food servers, housekeeping personnel, and maintenance people. Such ads may yield surprising results. If the volume of response for housekeeping personnel is insufficient to provide a suitable hiring base, the following sources may be investigated:

1. Local employment agencies
2. Flyers posted on community bulletin boards
3. Local church organizations
4. Neighborhood canvass for friends of recently hired employees
5. Direct radio appeals to local homemakers
6. Organizations for underprivileged ethnic minorities, and mentally disabled people.

If these sources do not produce the volume of applicants necessary to develop a staff, it may become necessary to search for employees in distant areas and to provide regular transportation for them to and from work. If aliens are hired, the department manager must take great care to ensure that they are legal residents of this country and that their green cards are valid. More than one hotel department manager has had an entire staff swept away by the Department of Immigration after hiring people who were illegal aliens. Such unfortunate action has required the immediate assistance of all available employees to fill in.

Processing Applicants

Whether you are involved in a mass hiring or in the recruiting of a single employee, a systematic and courteous procedure for processing applicants is essential. The efficient handling of lines of employees, courteous attendance, personal concern for employee desires, and reference to suitable departments for those unfamiliar with what the hotel or hospital has to offer all become earmarks for how the company will treat its employees. The key to proper handling of applicants is the use of a control system whereby employees are conducted through the steps of application, prescreening, and if qualified, reference to a department for interview.

Even though an employee may desire involvement in one classification of work, he or she may be hired for employment in a different department. Also, employees might not be aware of the possibilities available in a particular department at the time of application or may be unable to locate in desired departments at the time of mass hirings. Employees who perform well should therefore be given the opportunity to transfer to other departments when the opportunities arise.

No person may be denied the opportunity to submit application for employment for a position of his or her choosing. Not only is the law strict on this point, but companies in any way benefiting from interstate commerce may not discriminate in the hiring of people based on race, color, national origin, or religious preference. Although specific hours and days of the week may be specified, it is a generally accepted fact that hotels and hospitals must maintain personnel operations that provide the opportunity for people to submit applications without prejudice.

Prescreening Applicants

The prescreening interview is a staff function normally provided to all hotel or hospital departments by the human resources section of the organization. Prescreening is a preliminary interview process in which unqualified applicants-those applicants who do not meet the criteria for a job as specified in the job specification-special qualifications-are selected (or screened) out. For example, an applicant for a secretarial job that requires the incumbent to take shorthand and be able to type 60 words a minute may be screened out if the applicant is not able to pass a relevant typing and shorthand test.

If a candidate is screened out by the personnel section, he or she should be told the reason immediately and thanked for applying for employment. Applicants who are not screened out should either be referred to a specific department for interview or, if all immediate positions are filled, have their applications placed in a department pending file for future reference. All applicants should be told that hiring decisions will be made by individual department managers based on the best qualifications from among those interviewed. A suggested agenda for a prescreening interview is as follows:

1. The initial contact should be cordial and helpful. Many employees are lost at this stage because of inefficient systems established for handling applicants. 2. During the prescreening interview, try to determine what the employee is seeking, whether such a position is available, or, if not, when such a position might become available.
3. Review the work history as stated on the application to determine whether the applicant meets the obvious physical and mental qualifications, as well as important human qualifications such as emotional stability, personality, honesty, integrity, and reliability.
4. Do not waste time if the applicant is obviously not qualified or if no immediate position is available. When potential vacancies or a backlog of applicants exists, inform the candidate. Be efficient in stating this to the applicant. Always make sure that the applicant gives you a phone number in order that he or she may be called at some future date. Because most applicants seeking employment are actively seeking immediate work, applications more than 30 days old are usually worthless.
5. If at all possible, an immediate interview by the department manager should be held after screening. If this is not possible, a definite appointment should be made for the candidate's interview as soon as possible.

Interview

An interview should be conducted by a manager of the department to which the applicant has been referred. In ongoing operations, it is often wise to also allow the supervisor for whom the new employee will work to visit with the candidate in order that the supervisor may gain a feel for how it would be to work together. The supervisor's view should be considered, since a harmonious relationship at the working level is important. Although the acceptance of an employee remains a prerogative of management, it would be unwise to accept an employee into a position when the supervisor has reservations about the applicant.

Certain personal characteristics should be explored when interviewing an employee. Some of these characteristics are native skills, stability, reliability, experience, attitude toward employment, personality, physical traits, stamina, age, sex, education, previous training, initiative, alertness, appearance, and personal cleanliness. Although employers may not discriminate against race, sex, age, religion, and nationality, overall considerations may involve the capability to lift heavy objects, enter men's or women's restrooms, and so on. In a housekeeping (or environmental services) department, people should be employed who find enjoyment in housework at home. Remember that character and personality cannot be completely judged from a person's appearance. Also, it should be expected that a person's appearance will never be better than when that person is applying for a job.

Letters of recommendation and references should be carefully considered. Seldom will a letter of recommendation be adverse, whereas a telephone call might be most revealing. If it were necessary to select the most important step in the selection process, interviewing would be it. Interviewing is the step that separates those who will be employed from those who will not. Poor interviewing techniques can make the process more difficult and may produce a result that can be both frustrating and damaging for both parties. In addition, inadequate interviewing will result in gaining incorrect information, being confused about what has been said, suppression of information, and, in some circumstances, complete withdrawal from the process by the candidate.

The following is a well-accepted list of the steps for a successful interview process.

1. Be prepared. Have a checklist of significant questions ready to ask the candidate. Such questions may be prepared from the body of the job description. This preparation will allow the interviewer to assume the initiative in the interview.
2. Find a proper place to conduct the interview.The applicant should be made to feel comfortable.The interview should be conducted in a quiet, relaxing atmosphere where there is privacy that will bring about a confidential conversation.
3. Practice. People who conduct interviews should practice interviewing skills periodically. Several managers may get together and discuss interviewing techniques that are to be used.
4. Be tactful and courteous. Put the applicant at ease, but also control the discussion and lead to important questions.
5. Be knowledgeable. Be thoroughly familiar with the position for which the applicant is interviewing in order that all of the applicant's questions may be answered. Also, have a significant background knowledge in order that general information about the company may be given.
6. Listen. Encourage the applicant to talk.This may be done by asking questions that are not likely to be answered by a yes or no. If people are comfortable and are asked questions about themselves, they will usually speak freely and give information that specific

questions will not always bring out. Applicants will usually talk if there is a feeling that they are not being misunderstood.

7. Observe. Much can be learned about an applicant just by observing reactions to questions, attitudes about work, and, specifically, attitudes about providing service to others. Observation is a vital step in the interviewing process.

If the results of an interview are negative and rejection is indicated, the candidate should be informed as soon as possible. A pleasant statement, such as "Others interviewed appear to be more qualified," is usually sufficient. This information can be handled in a straightforward and courteous manner and in such a way that the candidate will appreciate the time that has been taken during the interview. When the results of the interview are positive, a statement indicating a favorable impression is most encouraging.

In many cases, reference checks are made only to verify that what has been said in the application and interview is in fact true. Many times applicants are reluctant to explain in detail why previous employment situations have come to an end. It is more important to hear the actual truth about a prior termination from the applicant than it is to hear that they simply have been terminated. Reference checks, in order of desirability, are as follows:

1. Personal (face-to-face) meetings with previous employers are the least available but provide the most accurate information when they can be arranged.
2. Telephone discussions are the next best and most often used approach. For all positions, an in-depth conversation by telephone between the potential new manager and the prior manager is most desirable;

otherwise a simple verification of data is sufficient to ensure honesty.

3. The least desirable reference is the written recommendation, because managers are extremely reluctant to state a frank and honest opinion that may later be used against them in court.

Applicants who are rated successful at an interview should be told that a check of their references will be conducted, and, pending favorable responses, they will be contacted by the personnel department within two days. Applicants who are currently employed normally ask that their current employer not be contacted for a reference check. This request should be honored at all times. Applicants who are currently working usually want to give proper notice to their current employers. If the applicant chooses not to give notice, chances are no notice will be given at the time he or she leaves your hotel.

In some cases, the applicant gives notice and, upon doing so, is "cut loose" immediately. If such is the case, the applicant should be told to contact the department manager immediately in order that the employee may be put to work as soon as possible.

There is no perfect interviewer, interviewee, or resultant hiring or rejection decision in regard to an applicant.We can only hope to improve our interviewing skills in order that the greatest degree of success in employee retention can be obtained.

Staff Orientation Programme

A carefully planned, concerned, and informational orientation program is significant to the first impressions that a new employee will have about the hospital or hotel in general and the housekeeping department in particular. Too often, a new employee is told where the work area and restroom are, given a cursory explanation of the job, then put to work. It is not uncommon to find managers putting employees to work who have not even been processed into the organization, an unfortunate situation that is usually discovered on payday when there is no paycheck for the new employee. Such blatant disregard for the concerns of the employee can only lead to a poor perception of the company. A planned orientation program will eliminate this type of activity and will bring the employee into the company with personal concern and with a greater possibility for a successful relationship.

A good orientation program is usually made up of four phases:

1. employee acquisition,
2. receipt of an employee's handbook,
3. tour of the facility, and
4. an orientation meeting.

Employee Acquisition

Once a person is accepted for employment, the applicant is told to report for work at a given time and place, and that place should be the personnel department. Preemployment procedures can take as much as one-half day, and department managers eager to start new employees to work should allow time for a proper employee acquisition into the organization. At this time it should be ensured that the application is complete and any additional information pertaining to employment history that may be necessary to obtain the necessary work permits and credentials is on hand. Usually the security department records the entry of a new employee into the staff and provides instructions regarding use of employee entrances, removing parcels from the premises, and employee parking areas. Application for work permits, and drug testing, will be scheduled where applicable. All documents required by the hotel's health and welfare insurer should be completed, and instructions should be given about immediately reporting accidents, no matter how slight, to supervisors.

Employee Handbook

The new employee should be provided with a copy of the hotel or hospital employee's handbook and should be told to read it thoroughly. Since the new housekeeping employee is not working just for the housekeeping department but is to become integrated as a member of the entire staff, reading this handbook is extremely important to ensure that proper instructions in the rules and regulations of the hotel are presented. The handbook should be developed in such a way as to inspire the new employee to become a fully participating member of the organization.

Tour of the Facility

Upon completion of the acquisition phase, a facility tour should be conducted for one or all new employees. For new facilities, access to the property should be gained within about one week before opening, and many new employees can be taken on a tour simultaneously. It is possible for employees to work in the hotel housekeeping department for years and never to have visited the showroom, dining rooms, ballrooms, or even the executive office areas.

A tour of the complete facility melds employees into the total organization, and a complete informative tour should never be neglected. For ongoing operations, after acquisition, the new employee may be turned over to a department supervisor, who becomes the tour director. An appreciation of the total involvement of each employee is strengthened when a facilities tour is complete and thorough. If necessary, the property tour might be postponed until after the orientation meeting; however, the orientation activity of staffing is not complete until a property tour is conducted.

Orientation Meeting

The orientation meeting should not be conducted until the employee has had an opportunity to become at least partially familiar with the surroundings. After approximately two weeks, the employee will have many questions about experiences, the new job, training, and the rules and regulations listed in the Property and Department Handbooks (see the following section on training). Employee orientation meetings that are scheduled too soon fail to answer many questions that will develop within the first two weeks of employment. The meeting should be held in a comfortable setting, with refreshments provided. It is usually conducted by the director of human resources and is attended by as many of the facility managers as possible.

Most certainly, the general manager or hospital administration members of the executive committee, the security director, and the new employees' department heads should attend. Each of these managers should have an opportunity to welcome the new employees and give them a chance to associate names with faces. All managers and new employees should wear name tags. In orientation meetings, a brief history of the company and company goals should be presented.

A planned orientation meeting should not be concluded without someone stressing the importance of each position. Every position must have a purpose behind it and is therefore important to the overall functioning of the facility. An excellent statement of this philosophy was once offered by a general manager who said, "The person mopping a floor in the kitchen at 3:00 A.M. is just as valuable to this operation as I am-we just do different things." The orientation meeting should be scheduled to allow for many questions. And there should be someone in attendance who can answer all of them.

Although the new employee will be gaining confidence and security in the position as training ends and work is actually performed, informal orientation may continue for quite some time. The formal orientation, however, ends with the orientation meeting (although the facility tour may be conducted after the meeting). Finally, it should be remembered that good orientation procedures lead to worker satisfaction and help quiet the anxieties and fears that a new employee may have. When a good orientation is neglected, the seeds of dissatisfaction are planted.

4

Training, Motivation and Evaluation of Staff

The efficiency and economy with which any department will operate will depend on the ability of each member of the organization to do his or her job. Such ability will depend in part on past experiences, but more commonly it can be credited to the type and quality of training offered. Employees, regardless of past experiences, always need some degree of training before starting a new job. Small institutions may try to avoid training by hiring people who are already trained in the general functions with which they will be involved. However, most institutions recognize the need for training that is specifically oriented toward the new experience, and will have a documented training program.

Some employers of housekeeping personnel find it easier to train completely unskilled and untrained personnel. In such cases, bad or undesirable practices do not have to be trained out of an employee. Previous experience and education should, however, be analyzed and considered in the training of each new employee in order that efficiencies in training can be recognized. If an understanding of department standards and policies can be demonstrated by a new employee, that portion of training may be shortened or modified. However, skill and ability must be demonstrated before training can be altered. Finally, training is the best method to communicate the company's way of doing things, without which the new employee may do work contrary to company policy.

First training of a new employee actually starts with a continuation of department orientation.When a new employee is turned over to the housekeeping or environmental services department, orientation usually continues by familiarizing the employee with department rules and regulations. Many housekeeping departments have their own department employee handbooks.

Many hotels use training aids in a conference room, or post messages on an employee bulletin board. Aside from the usual training aids such as chalkboards, bulletin boards, charts, graphs, and diagrams, photographs can supply clear and accurate references for how rooms should be set up, maids' carts loaded, and routines accomplished. Most housekeeping operations have films on guest contact and courtesy that may also be used in training. Motion pictures speak directly to many people who may not understand proper procedures from reading about them. Many training techniques may be combined to develop a well-rounded training plan.

Systematic Approach to Training

Training may be defined as those activities that are designed to help an employee begin performing tasks for which he or she is hired or to help the employee improve performance in a job already assigned. The purpose of training is to enable an employee to begin an assigned job or to improve upon techniques already in use. In hotel or hospital housekeeping operations, there are three basic areas in which training activity should take place: skills, attitudes, and knowledge.

Skills Training

A sample list of skills in which basic housekeeping employee must be trained follows:

1. *Bed making:* Specific techniques; company policy
2. *Vacuuming:* Techniques; use and care of equipment
3. *Dusting*: Techniques; use of products
4. *Window and mirror cleaning:* Techniques and products
5. *Setup awareness:* Room setups; what a properly serviced room should look like
6. *Bathroom cleaning*: Tub and toilet sanitation; appearance; methods of cleaning and results desired
7. *Daily routine*: An orderly procedure for the conduct of the day's work; daily communications
8. Caring for and using equipment: Housekeeper cart; loading
9. *Industrial safety:* Product use; guest safety; fire and other emergencies The best reference for the skills that require training is the job description for which the person is being trained.

Guidance in Attitudes

Employees need guidance in their attitudes about the work that must be done. They need to be guided in their thinking about rooms that may present a unique problem in cleaning. Attitudes among section housekeepers need to be such that, occasionally, when rooms require extra effort to be brought back to standard, it is viewed as being a part of rendering service to the guest who paid to enjoy the room.

Positive relationships with various agencies and people also need to be developed. The following is a list of areas in which attitude guidance is important:

1. The guest/patient
2. The department manager and immediate supervisor
3. A guestroom that is in a state of great disarray
4. The hotel and company
5. The uniform
6. Appearance
7. Personal hygiene

Setting Standards of Performance

The most important task of the trainer is to prepare new employees to meet standards. With this aim in mind, sequence of performance in cleaning a guestroom is most important in order that efficiency in accomplishing day-to-day tasks may be developed. In addition, the best method of accomplishing a task should be presented to the new trainee. Once the task has been learned, the next thing is to meet standards, which may not necessarily mean doing the job the way the person has been trained.

Knowledge Training

Areas of knowledge in which the employee needs to be trained are as follows:

1. Thorough knowledge of the hotel layout; employee must be able to give directions and to tell the guest about the hotel, restaurants, and other facilities
2. Knowledge of employee rights and benefits
3. Understanding of grievance procedure
4. Knowing top managers by sight and by name

Ongoing Training

There is a need to conduct ongoing training for all employees, regardless of how long they have been members of the department. There are two instances when additional training is needed:

(1) the purchase of new equipment, and

(2) change in or unusual employee behavior while on the job.

When new equipment is purchased, employees need to know how the new equipment differs from present equipment, what new skills or knowledge are required to operate the equipment, who will need this knowledge, and when. New equipment may also require new attitudes about work habits.

Employee behavior while on the job that is seen as an indicator for additional training may be divided into two categories: events that the manager witnesses and events that the manager is told about by the employees. Events that the manager witnesses that indicate a need for training are frequent employee absence, considerable spoilage of products, carelessness, a high rate of accidents, and resisting direction by supervisors. Events that the manager might be told about that indicate a need for training are that something doesn't work right, something is dangerous to work with, something is making work harder.

Although training is vital for any organization to function at top efficiency, it is expensive.The money and man-hours expended must therefore be worth the investment. There must be a balance between the dollars spent training employees and the benefits of productivity and high-efficiency performance.A simple method of determining the need for training is to measure performance of workers: Find out what is going on at present on the job, and match this performance with what should be happening.The difference, if any, describes how much training is needed.

In conducting performance analysis, the following question should be asked: Could the employee do the job or task if his or her life depended on the result? If the employee could not do the job even if his or her life depended on the outcome, there is a deficiency of knowledge. If the employee could have done the job if his or her life depended on the outcome, but did not, there is a deficiency of execution. Some of the causes of deficiencies of execution include task interference, lack of feedback, and the balance of consequences. If either deficiency of knowledge or deficiency of execution exists, training must be conducted.The approach or the method of training may differ, however.Deficiencies of knowledge can be corrected by training the employee to do the job, then observing and correcting as necessary until the task is proficiently performed. Deficiency of execution is usually corrected by searching for the underlying cause of lack of performance, not by teaching the actual task.

Training Methods

There are numerous methods or ways to conduct training. Each method has its own advantages and disadvantages, which must be weighed in the light of benefits to be gained. Some methods are more expensive than others but are also more effective in terms of time required for comprehension and proficiency that must be developed. Several useful methods of training housekeeping personnel are listed and discussed.

On-the-job Training

Using on-the-job training (OJT), a technique in which "learning by doing" is the advantage, the instructor demonstrates the procedure and then watches the students perform it.With this technique, one instructor can handle several students. In housekeeping operations, the instructor is usually a GRA who is doing the instructing in the rooms that have been assigned for cleaning that day. The OJT method is not operationally productive until the student is proficient enough in the training tasks to absorb part of the operational load.

Simulation Training

With simulation training, a model room is set up and used to train several employees.Whereas OJT requires progress toward daily production of ready rooms, simulation requires that the model room not be rented. In addition, the trainer is not productive in cleaning ready rooms. The advantages of simulation training are that it allows the training process to be stopped, discussed, and repeated if necessary. Simulation is an excellent method, provided the trainer's time is paid for out of training funds, and clean room production is not necessary during the workday.

Coach-pupil Method

The coach-pupil method is similar to OJT except that each instructor has only one student (a one-to-one relationship). This method is desired, provided that there are enough qualified instructors to have several training units in progress at the same time.

Lecture Method

The lecture method reaches the largest number of students per instructor. Practically all training programs use this type of instruction for certain segments. Unfortunately, the lecture method can be the dullest training technique, and therefore requires instructors who are gifted in presentation capabilities. In addition, space for lectures may be difficult to obtain and may require special facilities.

Conference Method

The conference method of instruction is often referred to as workshop training. This technique involves a group of students who formulate ideas, do problem solving, and report on projects. The conference or workshop technique is excellent for supervisory training.

Demonstrations

When new products or equipment are being introduced, demonstrations are excellent. Many demonstrations may be conducted by vendors and purveyors as a part of the sale of equipment and products. Difficulties may arise when language barriers exist. It is also important that no more information be presented than can be absorbed in a reasonable period of time; otherwise misunderstandings may arise.

Performance Appraisal

Whether you are conducting a training or a development program, suitable records of training progress should be maintained both by the training supervisor and the student. Periodic evaluations of the student's progress should be conducted, and successful completion of the program should be recognized. Public recognition of achievement will inspire the newly trained or developed employee to achieve standards of performance and to strive for advancement.

Once an employee is trained or developed and his or her satisfactory performance has been recognized and recorded, the person should perform satisfactorily to standards. Future performance may be based on beginning performance after training. If an employee's performance begins to fall short of standards and expectations, there has to be a reason other than lack of skills. The reason for unsatisfactory performance must then be sought out and addressed. This type of follow-up is not possible unless suitable records of training and development are maintained and used for comparison.

Although evaluation and performance appraisal for employees will occur as work progresses, it is not uncommon to find the design of systems for appraisal as part of organization and staffing functions. This is true because first appraisal and evaluation occurs during training, which is an activity of staffing. Once trainees begin to have their performance appraised, the methods used will continue throughout employment. As a part of training, new employees should be told how, when, and by whom their performances will be evaluated, and should be advised that questions regarding their performance will be regularly answered.

Initial employment should be probationary in nature, allowing the new employee to improve efficiency to where the designated number of rooms cleaned per day can be achieved in a probationary period (about three months). Should a large number of employees be unable to achieve the standard within that time, the standard should be investigated. Should only one or two employees be unable to meet the standard of rooms cleaned per day, an evaluation of the employee in training should either reveal the reason why or indicate the employee as unsuitable for further retention. An employee who, after suitable training, cannot meet a reasonable performance standard should not be allowed to continue employment. Similarly, an employee who has met required performance standards in the specified probationary period should be continued into regular employment status and thus achieve a reasonable degree of security in employment.

Training and Development

Recall that the definition of training is preparing a person to do a job for which he or she is hired or to improve upon performance of a current job. Development is preparing a person for advancement or to assume greater responsibility. The techniques are the same, but the end result is quite different.Whereas training begins after orientation of an employee who is hired to do a specific job, upon introduction of new equipment, or upon observation and communication with employees indicating a need for training, development begins with the identification of a specific employee who has shown potential for advancement.

Training for promotion or to improve potential is in fact development and must always include a much neglected type of training -supervisory training. Many forms of developmental training may be given on the property; other forms might include sending candidates to schools and seminars. Developmental training is associated primarily with supervisors and managerial development and may encompass many types of experiences.

Development of individuals within the organization looks to future potential and promotion of employees. Specifically, those employees who demonstrate leadership potential should be developed through supervisory training for advancement to positions of greater responsibility. Unfortunately, many outstanding workers have their performance rewarded by promotion but are given no development training. The excellent section housekeeper who is advanced to the position of senior housekeeper without the benefit of supervisory training is quickly seen to be unhappy and frustrated and may possibly become a loss to the department. It is therefore most essential that individual potential be developed in an orderly and systematic manner, or else this potential may never be recognized.

While undergoing managerial development, student and management alike should not lose sight of the primary aim of the program, which is the learning and potential development of the trainee, not departmental production. Even though there will be times that the trainee may be given specific responsibilities to oversee operations, clean guestrooms, or service public areas, advantage should not be taken of the trainee or the situation to the detriment of the development function. Development of new growth in the trainee becomes difficult when the training instructor or coordinator is not only developing a new manager but is also being held responsible for the production of some aspect of housekeeping operations.

Employee Motivation

Every person has different reasons for working. The reasons for working are as individual as the person. But, we all work because we obtain something that we need from work. The something we obtain from work impacts our morale and motivation and the quality of our lives. Here is the most recent thinking about what people want from work.

Some people work for love; others work for personal fulfillment. Others like to accomplish goals and feel as if they are contributing to something larger than themselves, something important. Some people have personal missions they accomplish through meaningful work. Others truly love what they do or the clients they serve. Some like the camaraderie and interaction with customers and coworkers. Other people like to fill their time with activity.

Some workers like change, challenge, and diverse problems to solve.

Whatever your personal reasons for working, the bottom line, however, is that almost everyone works for money. Whatever you call it: compensation, salary, bonuses, benefits or remuneration, money pays the bills. Money provides housing, gives children clothing and food, sends teens to college, and allows leisure activities, and eventually, retirement. To underplay the importance of money and benefits to people who work is a mistake.

Fair benefits and pay are the cornerstone of a successful company that recruits and retains committed workers. If you provide a living wage for your employees, you can then work on motivational issues. Without the fair, living wage, however, you risk losing your best people to a better-paying employer.

In today's turbulent, often chaotic, environment, commercial success depends on employees using their full talents. Yet in spite of the myriad of available theories and practices, managers often view motivation as something of a mystery. In part this is because individuals are motivated by different things and in different ways.

In addition, these are times when delayering and the flattening of hierarchies can create insecurity and lower staff morale. Moreover, more staff than ever before are working part time or on limited-term contracts, and these employees are often especially hard to motivate.

Advantages of Employee Motivation

A positive motivation philosophy and practice should improve productivity, quality, and service. Motivation helps people:

— achieve goals;

— gain a positive perspective;

— create the power to change;

— build self-esteem and capability,

— manage their own development and help others with theirs.

Disadvantages of Motivating Staff

There are no real disadvantages to successfully motivating employees, but there are many barriers to overcome.

Barriers may include unaware or absent managers, inadequate buildings, outdated equipment, and entrenched attitudes, for example:

— "We don't get paid extra to work harder."

— "We've always done it this way."

— "Our bosses don't have a clue about what we do."

— "It doesn't say that in my job description."

— "I'm going to do as little as possible without getting fired."

Such views will take persuasion, perseverance, and the proof of experience to break down.

Employee Motivation Action Checklist

This checklist is designed for managers with responsibilities for managing, motivating, and developing staff at a time when organizational structures and processes are undergoing continual change.

1. *Read the Gurus.* Familiarize yourself with Herzberg's hygiene theory, McGregor's X and Y theories and Maslow's hierarchy of needs. Although these theories date back some years, they are still valid today. Consult a digest to gain a basic understanding of their main principles; it will be invaluable for building a climate of honesty, openness, and trust.
2. *What Motivates You?* Determine which factors are important to you in your working life and how they interact. What has motivated you and demotivated you in the past? Understand the differences between real, longer-term motivators and short-term spurs.
3. *Find Out What Your People Want From Work* People may want more status, higher pay, better working conditions, and flexible benefits. But find out what really motivates your employees by asking them in performance appraisals, attitude surveys, and informal conversations what they want most from their jobs. Do people want, for example:
   - — more interesting work?
   - — more efficient bosses?
   - — more opportunity to see the end result of their work?

— greater participation?
— greater recognition?
— greater challenge?
— more opportunities for development?

4. *Walk the Job.* Every day, find someone doing something well and tell the person so. Make sure the interest you show is genuine without going overboard or appearing to watch over people's shoulders. If you have ideas as to how employees' work could be improved, don't shout them out, but help them to find their way instead. Earn respect by setting an example; it is not necessary to be able do everything better than your staff. Make it clear what levels of support employees can expect.
5. *Remove Demotivators.* Identify factors that demotivate staff - they may be physical (buildings, equipment) or psychological (boredom, unfairness, barriers to promotion, lack of recognition). Some of them can be dealt with quickly and easily; others require more planning and time to work through. The fact that you are concerned to find out what is wrong and do something about it is in itself a motivator.
6. *Demonstrate Support.* Whether your working culture is one that clamps down on mistakes and penalizes error or a more tolerant one that espouses mistakes as learning opportunities, your staff need to understand the kind and levels of support they can expect. Motivation practice and relationship building often falter because staff do not feel they are receiving adequate support.
7. *Be Wary of Cash Incentives.* Many people say they are working for money and claim in conversation that their fringe benefits are an incentive. But money actually comes low down in the list of motivators, and

it doesn't motivate for long after a raise. Fringe benefits can be effective in attracting new employees, but benefits rarely motivate existing employees to use their potential more effectively.

8. *Decide on an Action.* Having listened to staff, take steps to alter your organization's policies and attitudes, consulting fully with staff and unions. Consider policies that affect flexible work, reward, promotion, training and development, and participation.

9. *Manage Change.* Adopting policies is one thing, implementing them is another. If poor motivation is entrenched, you may need to look at the organization's whole style of management. One of the most natural of human instincts is to resist change even when it is designed to be beneficial. The way change is introduced has its own power to motivate or demotivate, and can often be the key to success or failure. If you:

   — tell - instruct or deliver a monologue - you are ignoring your staff's hopes, fears, and expectations;

   — tell and sell - try to persuade people - even your most compelling reasons will not hold sway over the long term if you don't allow discussion;

   — consult - it will be obvious if you have made up your mind beforehand;

   — look for real participation - sharing the problem solving and decision making with those who are to implement change - you can begin to expect commitment and ownership along with the adaptation and compromise that will occur naturally.

10. Understand Learning Preferences In their Manual of Learning Styles, Peter Honey and Alan Mumford distinguish four basic styles of learning:

— *activists:* like to get involved in new experiences, problems, or opportunities. They're not too happy sitting back, observing, and being impartial;

— *theorists*: are comfortable with concepts and theory. They don't like being thrown in at the deep end without apparent purpose or reason;

— *reflectors:* like to take their time and think things through. They don't like being pressured into rushing from one thing to another;

— *pragmatists:* need a link between the subject matter and the job in hand. They learn best when they can test things out.

As each of us learns with different styles, preferences, and approaches, your people will respond best to stimuli and suggestions that take account of the way they do things best.

11. *Provide Feedback.* Feedback is one of the most valuable elements in the motivation cycle. Don't keep staff guessing how their development, progress, and accomplishments are shaping up. Offer comments with accuracy and care, keeping in mind next steps or future targets.

How to Demonstrate Respect at Work

Ask anyone in your workplace what treatment they most want at work. They will likely top their list with the desire to be treated with dignity and respect. Popular songs tout the need for respect.

From Aretha Franklin:

"R-E-S-P-E-C-T

Find out what it means to me."

to Train:

"Everybody needs a little respect
Everybody needs a little time
Everybody needs a little respect
Everybody needs a little."

Everybody needs a little respect. You know when you have respect. You know when you don't. But what is respect really? And, how is respect demonstrated at work?

You can demonstrate respect with simple, yet powerful actions. These ideas will help you avoid needless, insensitive, unmeant disrespect, too.

— Treat people with courtesy, politeness, and kindness.

— Encourage coworkers to express opinions and ideas.

— Listen to what others have to say before expressing your viewpoint.

— Never speak over, butt in, or cut off another person.

— Use people's ideas to change or improve work. Let employees know you used their idea, or, better yet, encourage the person with the idea to implement the idea.

— Never insult people, name call, disparage or put down people or their ideas.

— Do not nit-pick, constantly criticize over little things, belittle, judge, demean or patronize. A series of seemingly trivial actions, added up over time, constitutes bullying.

— Treat people the same no matter their race, religion, gender, size, age, or country of origin. Implement policies and procedures consistently so people feel that they are treated fairly and equally. Treating people differently can constitute harassment or a hostile work environment.

— Include all coworkers in meetings, discussions, training, and events. While not every person can participate in every activity, do not marginalize, exclude or leave any one person out. Provide an equal opportunity for employees to participate in committees, task forces, or continuous improvement teams. Solicit volunteers and try to involve every volunteer.

— Praise much more frequently than you criticize. Encourage praise and recognition from employee to employee as well as from the supervisor.

There are many other ways to demonstrate respect at work. These ten constitute a solid foundation. Implemented consistently at work, these respectful actions help ensure a respectful, considerate, professional work place.

Ways to Show Appreciation to Employees

You can tell your colleagues, coworkers and employees how much you value them and their contribution any day of the year. Trust me. No occasion is necessary. In fact, small surprises and tokens of your appreciation spread throughout the year help the people in your work life feel valued all year long.

Looking for ideas about how to praise and thank coworkers and employees? Here are ten ways to show your appreciation to employees and coworkers.

— Praise something your coworker has done well. Identify the specific actions that you found admirable.

— Say "thank you." Show your appreciation for their hard work and contributions. And, don't forget to say "please" often as well. Social niceties do belong at work. A more gracious, polite workplace is appreciated by all.

— Ask your coworkers about their family, their hobby, their weekend or a special event they attended.

— Your genuine interest - as opposed to being nosey - causes people to feel valued and cared about.

— Offer staff members flexible scheduling for the holidays, if feasible. If work coverage is critical, post a calendar so people can balance their time off with that of their coworkers.

— Know your coworker's interests well enough to present a small gift occasionally. An appreciated gift, and the gesture of providing it, will light up your coworker's day.

— If you can afford to, give staff money. End of the year bonuses, attendance bonuses, quarterly bonuses and gift certificates say "thank you" quite nicely. — TechSmith staff received a percentage of their annual salary for their end of year bonus.

— Almost everyone appreciates food. Take coworkers or staff to lunch for a birthday, a special occasion or for no reason at all. Let your guest pick the restaurant.

— Create a fun tradition for a seasonal holiday.

— Bring in bagels, doughnuts or another treat for staff and coworkers. Offerings such as cookies or cupcakes, that you've baked personally, are a huge hit.

— Last, but not least, provide opportunity. People want chances for training and cross-training. They want to participate on a special committee where their talents are noticed. They like to attend professional association meetings and represent your organization at civic and philanthropic events.

These are many ways to show appreciation to employees and coworkers. Stretch your imagination. There are hundreds of other employee and coworker appreciation ideas just waiting to be found. They'll bring you success in employee motivation, employee recognition and in building a positive, productive workplace.

EVALUATION

Evaluation of personnel is an attempt to measure selected traits, characteristics, and productivity. Unfortunately, evaluations are generally objective in nature, and raters are seldom trained in the art of subjective evaluation. Initiative, self-control, and leadership ability do not lend themselves to measurement; therefore such characteristics are estimated. How well they are estimated depends to a great extent on the person doing the estimating. Two raters using the same form and rating the same person will probably arrive at different conclusions.

Certain policies on the use of evaluations should be established so that they are understood by both the person person doing the evaluating and the person being evaluated. These policies must be established and disseminated by management. Reliable evaluations require careful planning and take considerable time, skill, and work. An evaluation must be understood by the employee.

Evaluation should be used at the end of a probationary period, and the employee must understand at the beginning of the period that he or she will be observed and evaluated. Each item, as well as what impact the evaluation will have on future employment, should be explained to the employee. People undergoing periodic evaluations, such as at the end of one year's employment, should also know why evaluations are being conducted and what may result from the evaluation. In both situations, the evaluation should be used for counseling and guidance so that performance may be improved upon or corrected if necessary.

Certainly, strong points should be pointed out. An employee should be made aware of good as well as not-so-good evaluations. Evaluations should be made for a purpose and not for the sake of an exercise. They should ultimately be used as management tools. Evaluations should be developed to fit the policies of the particular institution using it and the particular position being evaluated.The same evaluation may not be suitable for every position.

5

Cleaning of the Hotel Premises

Cleanliness is the absence of dirt, including dust, stains, bad smells and clutter. Purposes of cleanliness include health, beauty, absence of offensive odor, avoidance of shame, and to avoid the spreading of dirt and contaminants to oneself and others. In the case of glass objects such as windows or windshields, the purpose can also be transparency. Washing is one way of achieving cleanliness, usually with water and often some kind of soap or detergent. In more recent times, since the germ theory of disease, it has also come to mean an absence of germs and other hazardous materials. In industry, certain processes such as those related to integrated circuit manufacturing, require conditions of exceptionally immaculate cleanliness which are achieved by working in cleanrooms.

Cleaning workers include janitors, maids, housekeeping cleaners, window washers, and rug shampooers-keep office buildings, hospitals, stores, apartment houses, hotels, and residences clean and in good condition. Some only do cleaning, while others have a wide range of duties. Janitors and cleaners perform a variety of heavy cleaning duties, such as cleaning floors, shampooing rugs, washing walls and glass, and removing rubbish. They may fix leaky faucets, empty trash cans, do painting and carpentry, replenish bathroom supplies, mow lawns, and see that heating and air-conditioning equipment works properly. On a typical day, janitors may wet- or dry-mop floors, clean bathrooms, vacuum carpets, dust furniture, make minor repairs, and exterminate insects and rodents. They also clean snow or debris from sidewalks in front of buildings and notify management of the need for major repairs. While janitors typically perform most of the duties mentioned, cleaners tend to work for companies that specialize in one type of cleaning activity, such as washing windows. Maids and housekeeping cleaners perform any combination of light cleaning duties to maintain private households or commercial establishments, such as hotels, restaurants, and hospitals, clean and orderly.

In hotels, aside from cleaning and maintaining the premises, maids and housekeeping cleaners may deliver ironing boards, cribs, and rollaway beds to guests' rooms. In hospitals, they also may wash bedframes, brush mattresses, make beds, and disinfect and sterilize equipment and supplies with germicides and sterilizing equipment. Janitors, maids, and cleaners use various equipment, tools, and cleaning materials. For one job they may need a mop and bucket, for another an electric polishing machine and a special cleaning solution. Improved building materials, chemical cleaners, and power equipment have made many tasks easier and less time consuming, but cleaning workers must learn the proper use of equipment and cleaners to avoid harming floors, fixtures, and themselves.

Cleaning supervisors coordinate, schedule, and supervise the activities of janitors and cleaners. They assign tasks and inspect building areas to see that work has been done properly, issue supplies and equipment, and inventory stocks to ensure that an adequate amount of supplies is present. They also screen and hire job applicants, train new and experienced employees, and recommend promotions, transfers, or dismissals.

Supervisors may prepare reports concerning the occupancy of rooms, hours worked, and department expenses. Some also perform cleaning duties. Cleaners and servants in private households dust and polish furniture; sweep, mop, and wax floors; vacuum; and clean ovens, refrigerators, and bathrooms. They also may wash dishes, polish silver, and change and make beds. Some wash, fold, and iron clothes; a few wash windows. General houseworkers also may take clothes and laundry to the cleaners, buy groceries, and perform many other errands.

Cleaning workers in hotels office and residential buildings often work in teams consisting of workers who specialize in vacuuming, picking up trash, and cleaning rest rooms, among other things. Supervisors conduct inspections to ensure that the building is cleaned properly and the team is functioning efficiently. Building cleaning workers usually work inside heated, well-lighted buildings. However, they sometimes work outdoors, sweeping walkways, mowing lawns, or shoveling snow.

Working with machines can be noisy, and some tasks, such as cleaning bathrooms and trash rooms, can be dirty and unpleasant. Janitors may suffer cuts, bruises, and burns from machines, handtools, and chemicals. They spend most of their time on their feet, sometimes lifting or pushing heavy furniture or equipment. Many tasks, such as dusting or sweeping, require constant bending, stooping, and stretching. As a result, janitors also may suffer back injuries and sprains.

Maintaining Floors

For making the hotel look beautiful, people choose a variety of flooring types. But, one thing that is equally significant is the fact that floors need to be maintained from time to time so as to make them more durable. When it comes to floor maintenance, the first thing that strikes mind is mopping and dusting of the floor at regular intervals. Mopping is extremely vital as it helps to protect the floor from dirt and mud.

A housemaid engaged in floor cleaning

Maintaining floors involves a long program consisting of multiple steps. First step starts with the cutting of extra-unwanted things that are glued to the floor with the help of a sharp edged knife. While cleaning, don't forget to clean those areas especially which are left out on a daily basis. One out of ten days should be kept for extra cleaning with a broom reaching out those areas, which remain untouched. Pick up a nice clean duster and get ready for the dusting work. Wipe off all the dust.

Locating the dirty areas is not enough. Once spotted these mud particles should be collected and thrown in the dustbin. The next step is proper stripping. For striping you need a couple of accessories like safety goggles, rubber gloves stripping pads, rubber boots for dust mopping, Towels Razor Scraper and 2 Clean Mops Low Speed Machine etc. So, if you want an exclusively unique look then you have to put in a little extra effort too towards hotel cleaning and that will also help you maintain that beautiful flooring.

Flooring Types

There is an exotic variety of floorings that you can choose from to decorate your hotel. Some are easy to install, totally hassle free while others might require tedious procedures to be followed. Some of the different flooring styles are Hardwood flooring, Softwood flooring, Custom flooring, Engineered and Laminate flooring. If you want to maintain a unique look you can go in for custom flooring, which can be shaped, according to your choice.

Hardwood flooring in itself has two sub types namely Unfinished and prefinished flooring. Unfinished flooring gives you the advantage of showing your own creativity and experiment with colors. It also requires some treatment to make its installation easier. There is a lot of scope of innovation. Prefinished flooring is easier to install and also comes with a long warranty period of about 15-25 years. It is more pocket friendly as no treatment in terms of milling or grilling is required. The entire finishing is done thus no scope for any changes.

Softwood flooring is apt for seasonal and environmental changes. Engineered floor style consists of multiple plywood. It can be used virtually in any space. Laminate flooring is apt for hotels where kids and pets make the hotel filthy. It is the concept of providing an extra covering and it makes use of a thin printed film, which is laminated. There are distinct styles of laminating one being glue and click together. Among the different flooring types, choose your flooring type keeping in mind the pros and cons of each type.

It's always a good idea to check with a flooring specialist for information on cleaning wood floors because certain treated flooring requires specific cleaning methods. However, one general wood-floor cleaner is a solution of 1/2 cup of apple cider vinegar in 1 gallon of warm water. Use a soft cloth with most of the moisture squeezed. Get on your hands and knees and wipe the floor without getting it wet. Then buff with a soft dry cloth to bring out the luster.

Sweep and damp mop using a gallon of water and a dash of dishwashing detergent, regularly to keep abrasive soil off the surface. Scrub as needed with a white nylon backed sponge to loosen stubborn, ground in soil. Nothing cleans as well as doing it on your hands and knees when you have time. Even no-wax floors eventually need waxing, this will help to prevent further deterioration.

Safe Floors

As important is the look, equally important is to maintain the safety of floorings. Safety and maintenance go hand in hand. To ensure safety, a proper maintenance plan needs to be worked out which consists of multifold steps like brooming, wetting the floor with water and then wiping it on regular intervals etc. For cleaning purpose, there are different methods that can be applied. A couple of methods used are No Buff method, Spray Buff method, Weekly Burnish Method etc.

No buff method is apt for small space floorings where it is difficult to use proper gadgets for maintenance. It is a style that goes in consistency with the latest floor finish developments. It demands less effort. Safety products that are required in this method are: Nu-Tral Cleaner, Speed Stripper and Blue Concentrate etc. Spray method is suitable for the deeply engraved soil. It also needs Buff 'N Clean spray buff. Both these two methods: No Buff method and Spray method are among the low maintenance types that demand less effort towards safety.

Among the high-class maintenance techniques we have Weekly Burnish Method and Daily Burnish Method. Weekly Burnish method requires the usual cleaning and dusting along with a weekly burnishing (which involves shining or glossing the surface to enhance its look). But for this method right finishing is a prerequisite. Daily burnishing insures an absolutely fantastic and shining appearance. Equipments required in these procedures are cleaners, restorer, stripper and finish products. If you like splendid flooring styles, then take care of their safety too as it is likely to affect your health and safety also by preventing slips and falls.

Interior Cleaning

Cleaning your hotel not only makes it shine like new and more hygienic but the process itself provides you with adequate physical exercise to keep you fit and healthy. It can be the positive point that you can meditate upon to prepare yourself to start and finish the arduous cleaning projects and its innumerable chores. Start cleaning your hotel with a positive attitude and you will find that you can actually enjoy the whole thing. Remember that you are doing the cleaning to give yourself an organized, tidy and sanitary environment and safe and healthy place to live in to your family. Taking help from the family members and even children will help you spend quality time with them.

Children can do small things like throwing things in the dustbin or collecting small but scattered things and put them in a box. This will also make them learn the need to keep things in place and keep their room tidy. They will also learn the value of keeping things organized. Besides the daily cleaning chores like sweeping the floors and cleaning kitchen countertop and washing dishes, you can do the rest of the work on weekends and major cleaning during vacations. Regular cleaning will keep your hotel shining and sparkling and you will take less time to give it a new look. Plan the most tiresome tasks for the specific fixed time of the day, when your energy level is highest and it should be essential for everybody in the hotel to clean and organize their own rooms to reduce your burden.

Most of the hotels these days are built with tiled floors. However, we may use different types of tiles for the purpose and many of us don't know about the appropriate tile cleaning methods. Following quick tips to clean your tiled floors will really be helpful for such people:

Tips for cleaning different types of floors

— The Linoleum floor can be cleaned with any solvent that is not chemical-based. Using aggressive scrubbing pad must be avoided. Avoid using alkaline products on these type of tiles as it causes the floor to turn yellow very soon.

— Whatever be the type of floor, test clean a small tiled area first and see the effects before using a floor cleanser on the entire floor.

— The floors with unglazed floor tiles can be cleaned by vacuum cleaners. They should be dusted very often. Use a mild detergent and little water to clean them.

— The Hardwood type of floors can be cleaned with oil soap and follow the instructions as mentioned on it. Before using oil soap, make sure that the tiles are free from dirt and dust. Use a moist mop or a sponge mop to apply on the floor but do not allow it to wet excessively. Let the floor dry before using it again. Regular cleaning of such floors will get rid of the scratches of the tiles.

— Sweep concrete floors often and use any degreaser or detergent based cleaner on them.

— The rubber tiled floors need to be cleaned at regular gaps with detergent and water.

Tile Cleaning

Cleaning Rusty Tile

— Rust stains on tile can be removed with kerosene.

Cleaning Ceramic Tile

— Before cleaning bathroom tiles, run the shower on hot for five minutes to steam the dirt loose.

— For stubborn stains, apply a paste of scouring powder and water and let sit for five minutes. Scrub with a nylon scrub pad, rinse and wipe dry.

— To keep the grout joints on tile countertops clean longer, wash with a solution of 1 to 2 tablespoons chlorine bleach in one quart of water. Dry thoroughly, then apply an acrylic sealer or three coats of lemon oil. Let dry one hour between coats.

— Remove mildew and make tiles sparkle by sponging with a solution of ammonia and water.

— Remove soot from fireplace tiles with a mixture of lemon juice and salt, then wash.

Cleaning Plastic Tile

— If bathroom walls are dull, wash the tiles with a solution of vinegar and water. Polish with a towel.

— Has a tile come loose? For a quick fix, put a little piece of chewing gum on each corner, use a warm iron to press it back into place.

Cleaning Porcelain

— Lighter fluid will remove most dark, stubborn stains from porcelain sinks and bathtubs.

Carpet Cleaning

People who understand carpet know that its immense success and consumer acceptance is not due to chance. Few construction materials offer the advantages that carpet does. Carpet is colorful, comfortable and yet easy to maintain. Even though it appears expensive, it is often the most economical choice for floor covering. Carpet and rugs found on the floors of residences and commercial buildings still represent a substantial investment. In light of this, is it not wise to maintain them correctly?

Like all textile materials, the beauty and life of a carpet depends largely on the care that it is given. Proper maintenance can add years of attractive life. Specific maintenance procedures for carpet are determined by where the carpet is installed. In general, proper maintenance involves regular vacuuming and periodic cleaning by methods such as hot water extraction, shampooing, bonnet cleaning, foam cleaning, etc.

Regular vacuuming is essential as it removes particulate soil that damages the fibers. Vacuuming maintains the surface appearance of a carpet and keeps the level of soil in the pile at an acceptable level. Vacuuming should be done at least once every two weeks, preferably once each week and even twice per week in soiled or heavily trafficked areas. It is important to use a well-maintained, good quality vacuum. Vacuuming removes only particulate soil and surface dirt; therefore, other methods of cleaning are periodically required to improve the appearance of the carpet. Wet cleaning methods are better for removing oils, greases and other forms of matter that cause soiling on carpet. These methods are mostly used by professional cleaners and trained personnel, but smaller, less powerful units, can also be rented for use by customers.

It has been said that ignorance is bliss. Sometimes, maybe, but not always. Before having a carpet cleaned, you may find it helpful to understand some of the carpet cleaning methods. The best method for cleaning a particular carpet is dependent on a range of factors. All carpet cleaning methods offer various advantages, but also have some limitations. No single method is superior to all others. Properly performed under appropriate conditions, each method can provide satisfactory results. Often, several methods can be combined to achieve the desired results. The following are some of the more prevalent carpet cleaning methods.

— *Hot Water Extraction or "Steam" Cleaning.* In this method, hot water cleaning solution is sprayed on the carpet and immediately extracted by a wet vacuum. Extraction equipment can be portable or truck-mounted, the latter being more powerful in terms of spray pressure, heating capabilities and power of the vacuum pumps. Hot water extraction is often referred to as "steam" cleaning. In actuality this is a misnomer as the temperature of the heated solution never reaches the point to generate steam.

— *Shampooing.* In this process, the cleaning solution is showered onto the carpet through several openings in a circular brush. The rotary action of the brush whips the detergent into a foam and provides agitation or rubbing action on the carpet. This suspends the soil, and the wet/dry vacuuming that follows removes it.

— *Bonnet Cleaning.* This method resembles the shampooing process described above. It employs a rotary floor machine on the bottom of which is attached a round absorbent pad. The detergent is sprayed directly on the carpet. As the machine is operated, the shag pad rotates on the carpet. This removes the soil as it is absorbed on the shag pad. The shag pad can also be moistened with detergent. When one side of the pad becomes soiled, the pad is reversed until both sides are soiled, at which time it is replaced.

— *Foam Cleaning.* This system uses detergent in the form of a foam. Machines are available that generate foam, which is agitated on the carpet by brushes. The foam is then removed, with trapped soil, by an extraction-vacuum pickup.

— *Dry (Absorbent Compound) Cleaning.* In this process the cleaning agent, an absorbent dry compound is sprinkled on the carpet and worked into the pile by a machine. It is vacuumed off after about half an hour, removing the soil suspended by the compound.

Vacuuming alone, although essential, cannot maintain the appearance of a carpet at an acceptable level for long. Depending on various factors, the appearance of any carpet will ultimately reach an unacceptable level. At that stage, cleaning is necessary by one of the methods mentioned above. The frequency of such cleaning will depend on a carpet's use conditions, soil conditions, fiber type, constructional specifications, color, etc. In general, residential carpet requires cleaning within one to one and one-half years; certainly before two years of use.

Do-It-Yourself Cleaning

Like most decisions, the choice between having a carpet cleaned professionally and D-I-Y cleaning is based frequently on financial considerations. Electing to use a rental unit rather than a professional cleaner may be penny wise and pound foolish. Before deciding to do it yourself, several points should be considered.

Contrary to common belief, carpet cleaning is an intricate process. When spots, stains and traffic patterns have made carpet unsightly, cleaning by D-I-Y methods may not enhance the appearance to the desired level. Consumers in most cases have had little or no previous experience operating the machines. Therefore, there is a good possibility of misuse and/or overuse. Machines can be rented for D-I-Y cleaning that utilize one of the various methods already mentioned. Shampooing machines, for example, leave some residue on the carpet. If the carpet is shampooed many times the residue can accumulate leading to various problems, such as severe foaming on later cleaning, stickiness etc.

Rental machines that use hot water extraction cleaning are the most popular for residential use. Successful cleaning by these machines is largely dependent on the experience of the operator. Improper use can leave the carpet overly wet, causing possible backing delamination, odor from development of mold-mildew-fungi, cellulosic browning, color run, shrinkage, and other related problems. This can happen especially in areas of repeated, high volume use, or "traffic lanes". One or two passes of the cleaning wand may not be sufficient to enhance the appearance of such areas. Attempts to clean them over and over again can cause overwetting and its attendant problems. D-I-Y cleaning by the dry-absorbent compound method will not cause such problems as overwetting, color run, shrinkage, etc. But it, too, can mean some headaches. If the final vacuuming operation is not thorough, some of the powder will be left in the carpet pile. With repeated cleanings, enough cleaning compound can accumulate to cause some discoloration by its own presence. The obvious conclusion is that carpet cleaning by D-I-Y methods is not a substitute for professional cleaning. It can, at best, merely postpone the need or reduce the frequency of professional cleanings. Rental units lack adequate power, and consumers usually lack the expertise to succeed in properly maintaining carpet and prolonging its attractive life.

Selecting the Right Carpet Cleaner

Having established that professional carpet cleaning is essential for extending a carpet or rug's attractive life, the next question is how does one go about choosing the right person or firm to do the job? There is no magical, single method for carpet cleaning. All methods have advantages as well as disadvantages. Moreover, different people can achieve different results while cleaning the same carpet with identical equipment. No method can compensate for an inept operator. Therefore, it is more important to select the right cleaner than the right cleaning method.

Not all cleaners are alike. In fact, the difference in the quality of service from one cleaner to another can be astounding. However, with so many claims, counterclaims and a diversion of equipment and technology available, how do you go about choosing the right person or firm? It can be difficult because there are so many choices available.

Furniture Cleaning

Most of the time that we spend in our hotels is spent walking and sitting. Yet, while people clean their floors and carpets daily, they often forget to clean their furniture. Constant neglect can make your furniture look like a vintage piece much earlier than you would have anticipated. To avoid this, we are giving some furniture cleaning tips here that will make the entire process, feel like a breeze:

— *Cleaning stained furniture:* Apply first a dry solvent cleaner to discolor the stain of your furniture. Then apply an oil-based grease on the same area. Now reapply the same solvent that you applied before and leave it for some time.

— *Cleaning woven furniture:* Dust your woven furniture or vacuum on daily basis. You can use sponge and water also to wipe the dust on the woven furniture. To protect the weaves, use a light coat of any furniture finish polish.

— *Cleaning courtyard furniture*: Take a solution which is a mixture of bleach and detergent in 5:1 ratio and spray it on your courtyard furniture ad leave it for an hour. Then rinse well using running water from a hose. Let it dry for couple of hours before using it.

— *Cleaning wooden furniture*: Use a diluted mild detergent based cleaner on your wooden furniture with the help of a sponge. Then clean it off with water using sponge to get back the shining effect of your wooden furniture.

— *Cleaning leather furniture:* If your leather furniture is of pigment-dye-based, you can clean it by yourself by a wet, soft cloth. But if it is of aniline-dye-based, use proper leather cleaner. Avoid using too many chemical based cleansers to clean your furniture.

— *Cleaning Plastic Furniture:* Plastic furniture generally needs a simple cleaning procedure. Just wash it with mild detergent and water and wipe it with a soft cloth.

Cleaning Painted Walls

No matter how much you take care of your walls and that they are recently painted, they do get dirty and dusty very easily. Here are some tips to clean walls painted recently and doors to give a new shine to your hotel without spending money:

- Cove the floor and immovable furniture in the room with old sheets and newspapers so that they don't get dirty from all the cleaning, falling dust and drippings of soap solutions.
- If your walls have been painted already, all you have to do to clean them is to clean the cobwebs first and then dust them well using a brush or soft cloth rag.
- If the paint is washable, then dip the sponge in a cleaning solution and squeeze it well and clean the wall from top the bottom. Then use a dry clean rag to dry-wipe the wall.
- Clean shower walls by spraying phosphoric acid cleaner on them and then wiping it off using a soft cloth rag or a sponge. This will remove all the dust and deposits on the walls. Then use a hand sprayer to spray any citrus-based solution to remove the soap scrum from the wall and then wipe it off using a sponge.
- Wear eye protective gear as protection for your eyes before starting the entire wall cleaning process.
- Damp walls and moisture-ridden walls need more ventilation and air circulation, so keep windows open during summers. However, in monsoons and winters, windows should remain closed so that humidity cannot make your walls damper.
- Use a dry clean cloth rag to wipe off the dust from the doors first and then use a wet cloth for additional cleanliness. Apply one coat of oil wood to keep your doors in good condition.

Cleaning Windows and Glass

A beautiful window view can make up your day in the morning but a misty or dirty window can keep you from enjoying the beauty of Nature and count your blessings as you start your day. So, if you want to enjoy the beauty of a rising sun, lapping waves of the ocean, snow-capped pine trees or exotic flowers of your garden, we will advise you to go through these simple tips to clean your windows and glasses. These tips are easy to follow too:

— Most of the people use a wet cloth to clean their papers but it can leave stains on glass panes.

— Paper towels are best to clean windows, glasses and mirrors.

— To clean water stains, use any good glass cleaner and steel wool to scrub them off gently.

— Glasses to block off sunrays are best cleaned by spraying detergent solution on them and then wipe it off using paper towels.

— Clean interior automotive windows by spraying a mild detergent based cleaner on them and then washing them thoroughly until the cleaner washes off.

— Clean aquarium from inside often using a scrubber pad to prevent the growth of algae and fungi. Tough stains can be scraped off using a plastic blade. In the end, use a cloth to sparkle clean the glass from both the sides.

Bedroom Cleaning

While we may be doing an excellent job of maintaining bedrooms, occasionally we need to do more than maintenance. Take the time to review what goes into a bedroom intense cleanup.

1. *Grab your supplies.*This is the most important step. Having all of your supplies together before you begin means no distractions in the middle of cleaning up. Everything is handy when you need it.
2. *Put all items that do not belong in the living room in a container.* Do not try to pick up each item and place it where it belongs. Even if you don't get distracted you will waste time running to all ends of the house multiple times.
3. *Tackle the couch.*Brush off the cushions. Retrieve any missing items from the depths of the couch. Brush off the dirt from the interior of the couch onto the floor. Replace and fluff the pillows.
4. *Dust down the coffee table and arrange its contents properly.* The goal here is to quickly brush off the table and neatly stack its contents. We're not shining the furniture meticulously, or alphabetizing coffee table books.
5. *Neatly arrange the magazines and books.* Don't try to weed out magazines and books that you've been thinking about storing or tossing. Just arrange them neatly and move on.
6. *Vacuum or sweep up the floor.* Don't move furniture to do so. Don't try to vacuum the pillows and couch. Leave these more in depth items for when you have more time. Do, however, remember to get the dirt we brushed out of the interior of the couch.
7. *Put away your dust rag and vacuum or broom.* Take a few moments to enjoy, and take some time for yourself. If you have a few minutes leftover after vacuuming, grab the container and take the missing items to their homes. It will probably only take a few minutes but save you time tomorrow morning.
8. *Dust down the living room ceiling and corners of walls in.* Determine if the walls need washed in dirty spots.

Spot wash, remembering air vents, doorknobs, doors, and switch plates.

9. ***Dust and clean all art and photographs along the walls in the living room.*** Be careful when cleaning framed art and photographs. Never spray cleanser or water onto the frame. The liquid can seep behind the glass and damage the pictures. Instead lightly wet a clean cloth to wipe the frame and glass.

10. *Dust and clean the ceiling fan in the living room.* There is nothing more embarrassing than turning on a ceiling fan and having large chunks of dust fall down on your guest's head. Use this living room cleaning time to dust down the fan and fan blades. You may need to use a gentle cleanser like Murphy's Oil Soap. Take down any light fixtures and gently wash and dry them before replacing.

11. *Take down draperies, curtains, and blinds to wash or have cleaned according to the manufacturer's directions.* Vacuum and clean windowsills and corners. Wash the insides and outsides of the windows. Take down and rinse off the screens of the living room windows, before replacing.

12. *Dust and clean out the couches and chairs.* Use a vacuum cleaner with attachment to clean out couch crevices. Check to make sure none of your missing items have found their way into the abyss of the couch. Clean slipcovers, accent pillows, etc. in the living room. Use an upholstery attachment on a rug shampoo machine to clean soiled couches and chair surfaces if needed. If a light cleaning is needed use upholstery spot cleaner. Test in a hidden area first.

13. *Dust down and clean all accent lamps and knickknacks in the living room.* Use a vacuum attachment or duster to clean the lampshades, lamps, and any extra decorative items.

14. *Remove books from bookshelves.* Dust down the books and the shelves. If your collection of books is overflowing, it might be time to donate, trash, or sell. Too many books weighing down shelves can give a living room the appearance of being cluttered.
15. *Dust down accent tables and your living room's entertainment center.* Unplug and dust down all the electronics. Check cords for fraying and wear. Dust down the television screen.
16. *Clean the carpets and rugs. If your carpets and rugs are heavily soiled it may be time to call a professional.* You can also rent cleaning machines to use. Be sure to ask for one with an upholstery attachment. If your carpets are only lightly soiled vacuuming and spot treating may be all that is necessary.
17. *Take the time to clean the doormats inside and outside your doorways. Wipe them down.* Dust them off. Whatever needs to happen so that shoes don't transfer the dirt of your mat to your home. Double check that your mats are still in good condition to protect your carpets.

Kitchen Cleaning

Cleaning the kitchen, bathroom and living room is even more difficult because of the heavy traffic in the area. But sanitation and hygiene is essential to keep healthy and fit. Most of us have heard from our elders that most of the illnesses and diseases breed in dirty kitchens. So, here are some easy steps to clean your kitchen:

— Wipe out the spills over the kitchen tiles at the earliest possible. Use soft detergent for this purpose.

— The light fixtures in the kitchen get more dust, dirt and grime than the ones in the other rooms. Use a wet scrubber to clean the grease on the lights of your kitchen.

— *Cleaning Refrigerators:* The enamel-coated surface of your refrigerator is easy to clean regularly with an all-purpose cleaner. Use a soft cloth or a sponge to remove the tough stain. Avoid using tough cleansers. The humid top surface of your refrigerator has to be cleaned with a liquid dish washing cleaner. To clean the racks of your refrigerator, again use a mild cleanser with a sponge.

— *Cleaning Stovetops:* Dismantle before cleaning your stove and keep the top parts and the rings aside. Use a dishwasher to wash the body of the stove and use a soft cloth to whip to get the spotless effect. Soak the rings in a detergent solution for some time and rub it with a mesh made out of plastic, then wash away the dirt by holding the stove parts in running water. Dry for some time before using.

— *Glassware cleaning:* Use lukewarm water to clean the glassware and let it dry normally.

— *Oven racks cleaning:* Cover your oven racks and soak them for overnight with ammonia. The next morning, wash them up with dish soap.

— *Cleaning kitchen exhaust*: To clean the dirt that is powerful and tough, apply a mixture of baking soda and water on it and let it soak for about couple of hours. Now, clean with white vinegar.

Here are ten money and time saving tips to help you in your kitchen.

1. Use those leftover slivers of soap to cut expenses! Cut a small pocket in a sponge and place small slivers of leftover soap into it for a sudsy washing sponge.

2. Hold a scouring pad underneath a sponge when scrubbing. This will give you a better grip and protect your hands.

3. Save time on the dinner dishes. Before serving dinner, run a sink full of very hot soapy water. When everyone is finished eating dinner, tell them to wash and rinse their own plate.
4. Use a paint scraper or putty knife to remove baked on or cemented goo from stovetops, countertops or floors.
5. Use a toothbrush to scrub hard to reach surfaces such as behind and on faucets.
6. Baking soda makes an excellent scouring powder.
7. By keeping a spoon rest on the stove, you'll avoid a lot of messy clean-ups.
8. Place sticky (honey, syrup, molasses and oil) containers on plastic lids in the cupboard or fridge to avoid sticky messes.
9. To get odors out of plastic containers, place crumpled newspaper inside the container and seal it overnight.
10. Keep a fillable wand near the kitchen sink and when you have a few spare minutes, wash a few dishes with the wand. This may help you cut down on doing full loads of dishes.

Following are some ideas to freshen up that kitchen with a very limited budget.

1. Repaint those cabinets! Unless you have high quality wood cabinets, chances are they could use some rejuvenation, and painted finishes are very hot! There are many techniques you can easily learn to give your kitchen cabinets an expensive designer look. Crackling, faux finishing, and glazing are all quite simple and cost effective.
2. Paint those walls! These days our kitchens are the hub of the home, and we all feel more comfortable in rooms that offer mood and character. If you have

wood cabinets, colour on the walls will make the wood appear richer, and will emphasise your accessories.

3. Make carved look molding and appliqués. There are several techniques for creating beautiful moldings and architectural embellishments for very little money. You can either use joint compound and a cake-decorating bag to create beautiful designs on plain wood strips, then prime and paint

4. Use fabric in your kitchen. Years ago, there was a belief that you shouldn't use fabric in a kitchen because of the grease and food splatters, and the difficulty cleaning. Nowadays, most fabrics can be thrown in the washer and dryer, so go ahead and use it! It softens the kitchen, can add romance or charm, and makes it feel like a warm connection to the rest of your house, instead of a cold utilitarian space. Curtains or valances, appliance covers, and table runners all can be easily stitched at home. (Or fused with an iron and hem tape available at your sewing or craft store.) Fabric does not have to be expensive either. Flat twin sheets are always a great value, and can be gotten on sale for as little as 3 dollars. Keep an eye out at garage sales for sheets, quilts, tablecloths, and even clothing that have your homes colour schemes.

Bathroom Cleaing

Cleaning the bathroom can be a thankless, dirty, but necessary job. Explore ideas for quickly cleaning the bathroom with thorough methods and timesaving products. Check out organizational ideas for the bathroom that leave a cramped medicine cabinet a thing of the past.

Cleaning a toilet can be a very disgusting chore, but at least it's uncomplicated, right? Actually there is a right way to begin cleaning a toilet. The right way prevents the spread of bacteria and viruses. The right way of cleaning a toilet also saves time and energy. Find out the right way to get your toilet clean.

Here's How:

— *Remove everything from around the toilet.* Cleaning the toilet is a messy job, and there's always the chance of splashing cleanser or toilet water outside of the actual toilet. Prevent extra cleanup by removing all excess items from around the toilet. Don't forget to remove anything on top of the tank to prevent dropping items into the bowl during cleaning.

— *Flush and add cleaning solution.* Flush the toilet with the lid down to prevent splashing or spraying. Add your choice of powdered, liquid, or gel cleanser to the bowl. Try to apply the cleaner as close to the toilet rim as possible to prevent diluted cleanser.

— *Clean the exterior of the toilet.* While the cleansing solution soaks into the toilet grime in the bowl, clean the outside of the toilet. Start at the top to prevent dripping on already clean surfaces. Spray the tank, handle, and tank edges with cleaner and wipe down. Next do the outside lid of the toilet. Finally wipe down the entire bowl. Start with the sides and front before cleaning the bottom edges of the toilet where it meets the floor.

— *Clean the toilet seat.* The toilet seat should never be neglected. It is the part of the toilet that comes into actual contact with people, and it needs to be cleaned thoroughly. Raise the seat. Spray the seat, inside lid and the rim of the toilet with cleanser. Wipe down the lid, seat, and hinges at the back of the toilet seat. Some toilets have hinges that will pop open to allow better access for cleaning.

— *Clean the inside of the toilet bowl.* Begin cleaning the bowl from the top down. Always begin scrubbing under the rim first. Look under the rim to get all the stains and grime scrubbed away. Next scrub the bowl. Finally scrub the hole at the bottom of the toilet. Flush the toilet with the lid down.

— *Wipe up any drips or spills.* Wipe up any drips of cleanser or water that may have occurred. Put away tools and trash. Replace the items removed in step 1. Enjoy a clean toilet.

Restroom Cleaning Systems

Customers expect managers to keep restrooms clean, and yet the end result year after year is that managers are failing. The technology of restroom cleaning is changing, however, giving managers an opportunity to be environmentally friendly in selecting chemicals to support the evolving technology. It is now possible for housekeeping managers to have the best of all worlds - to integrate highly productive equipment with environmentally friendly and cost-effective products to enhance the level of cleanliness in restrooms. Today's marketplace of custodial equipment affords housekeeping managers many advantages in cleaning restrooms, compared with the days of the traditional mop, bucket and wringer. The traditional method, though still in use, is increasingly falling behind the new technologies.Some new systems are simple, while others are more complex, but most systems enhance the performance of cleaning chemicals and all while enabling managers to minimize complaints by effectively cleaning restrooms.

Vapour cleaning

These restroom cleaning systems are becoming increasingly popular. The systems use no chemicals.

Instead, they use a tank that superheats the water, and operators spray the resulting steam onto the dirty areas with a special wand that features an applicator to which cleaning towels might be attached. The operator wipes all surfaces with the superheated vapor, changing the cloth as it becomes soiled. The units also have special heads that allow for crevice cleaning. In addition to using these units for cleaning restrooms, cleaning crews also can use them for cleaning kitchens because the steam easily breaks down the grease. Also, when using the wand and towel attachment, the units might be effective in cleaning dirt off walls.

Manufacturers of some of these systems claim that the units require no chemicals, but housekeeping managers should familiarize themselves with the claims and the infection-control needs of their facility. Also, operators need to be aware that the vapor is hot and that handles of some wands might become hot. As a result, they will need to wear appropriate personal protective equipment. Several manufacturers now market restroom cleaning kits that might include a cleaning cart, a bucket and a series of extension handles with associated specialized mop heads and attachments. The cart has space for storing cleaning supplies and paper products. Increasingly, crews are replacing old cotton-string mops with microfiber flat mops that are easier to use, lighter and enable aggressive cleaning of the surface. Some advocates of microfiber cleaning cloths say that the cloths eliminate or mitigate the need for cleaning chemicals. Realistically, crews often can enhance their cleaning efforts in restrooms by applying the appropriate chemicals during the cleaning process.

Powered cleaning equipment

Specialized power washers for cleaning restrooms have been available for several years now. Generally, the power washer is cart-mounted for carrying limited cleaning supplies and might come in various sizes. Basically, after the floor has been swept, the unit allows the operator to power-wash the restroom from ceiling to floor and to air dry the room before use. These units have specialized chemicals, applied through a solution pick-up hose, that afford deep cleaning and drying of surfaces without leaving spots, much like an effective dishwashing agent. More advanced units not only can allow an operator to power spray a room but can also pick up the residue solution after cleaning to minimize the time that a restroom is out of service.

When using these units, operators need use all appropriate safety precautions. For example, crews should not spray chemicals into electrical outlets, and they should make sure that paper goods are adequately protected from solution overspray. When used correctly, these units really do deliver deep cleaning to restrooms. Manufacturers have provided a new generation of equipment for housekeeping managers to specify to improve the level of restroom cleaning in their facilities. Several can help minimize the use of chemicals.

Housekeeping managers who want to curtail complaints concerning their facilities' restrooms and minimize the impact of cleaning chemicals and processes on the environment have more options than ever today. They can achieve these goals by learning about those options.Today's environmentally friendly chemicals and equipment are increasingly cost competitive, have increased efficacy, limit damage to the environment and minimize costs to an organization for disposal of chemicals. In more cases than ever, it is a winning combination to clean restrooms with green chemicals and equipment that can solve restroom cleaning complaints and control costs at the same time.

Infection control

Housekeeping practices, if performed correctly through educational presentations, will create an area suitable for patient, visitor and healthcare worker to enter and be comfortable within the confines of the environment. The proper maintenance of a health care facility increases the awareness of other employees of the necessity of good sanitary practices. Good housekeeping practices increase moral and public relations. No one wants to work in an area that smells or is dirty. Sanitation depends upon cleaning thoroughness. There should be procedures in writing to fit each area of the facility such as walls, floors, windows, beds, furniture, draperies, carpets, waste containers, bathrooms, equipment, stairs, elevators, special-care equipment and handling of infectious waste for disposal.

Toilet Cleaning Tools

Automatic or Drop-In Toilet Cleaners: Automatic or Drop-In Toilet cleaners usually consist of a disc of cleaner that you deposit into the toilet tank. Some other models suspend from the toilet tank or rim of the toilet. They automatically dispense cleaning solution into the water when the toilet is flushed. An automatic cleaner is easy to use and easy to maintain. The toilet will still need to be scrubbed occasionally. These cleaners aren't a good idea if you have pets or children who are likely to have access.

Powder Toilet Cleaners: Powder Toilet cleaners are designed to scrub a toilet without scratching it. These cleaners are a good choice when staining of the toilet bowl is an issue. If you have rust or water deposit stains in your toilet bowl, using a powder cleanser offers enough scrubbing power without scratching your toilet. Be careful not to scratch the surfaces of the toilet, which will allow future staining to occur more easily. Abrasive cleaners also require the use of an additional brush.

Toilet Brushes: Toilet brushes are bristle brushes that usually come with a storage container. Many companies market the toilet brushes to match bathroom decor. A good toilet brush with stiff all-plastic brush and bristles does a great job at scrubbing a toilet. Don't choose a brush with bristles attached to wire. This can damage toilets. A toilet brush needs to be thoroughly disinfected and/or kept away from areas where it could cross contaminate with bacteria. Cheap brushes can also damage the toilet.

Eye and Hand Protection: Even the most experienced toilet cleaner can occasionally splash water and or cleaner during a good scrubbing. Protect your eyes with goggles and your hands with gloves. This is one of the filthiest places in your home. You do not want the contents or the cleaner anywhere near your eyes and hands.

Disposable Toilet Cleaning Systems: Almost every cleaning product company has some form of a disposable toilet cleaning system on the market. This systems allow you to have disposable prefilled cleaning heads, or automatic cleanser triggers that keep you from relying on a reusable brush and separate cleanser. These systems save time because there is little cleanup. The cleaning systems work fairly well, although toilets with staining may still need a brush. Disposable cleaners and cloths aren't friends to the environment.

Paper Towels vs. Rags: Sometimes it seems as though the outside has become dirtier than the bowl. Using paper towels, rags, or sponges along with a spray cleaner will get the outside as gleaming as the bowl.

Paper towels are able to be thrown away. There is no risk of contaminating other surfaces or laundry. Paper towels aren't the most environmentally friendly choice for cleaning. Use rags if you prefer, but wash right away in hot water. Otherwise, go with paper towels, and never use sponges.

Effective Steps for Bathroom Cleaning

You too can overcome the bathroom blues by following these simple and effective twelve steps.

1. Remove the knick knacks and place them in the hallway.
2. Remove the throw rugs and shake them out. Put them in the laundry to be cleaned if needed.
3. Sweep or vacuum the floor.
4. Spray the counter top and let your cleaner do the work.
5. Spray the mirror and wipe it down.
6. Spray the toilet with cleaner inside and out. Let the cleaner sit.
7. Go back to the counter top. Scrub and wipe it down.
8. Spray the bath tub and shower down.
9. Scrub the inside of the toilet with a brush. Flush the toilet to rinse the bowl. Wipe down the outside. Don't forget the place behind the seat and the outside of the toilet bowl and base.
10. Scrub the tub down and rinse.
11. If you have linoleum or tile, mop the floor. If the room is small, you can spray your cleaner directly onto the floor and wipe it up with a sponge or cleaning cloth. Let dry for ten to fifteen minutes.

12. Put back the rugs and knick knacks. Check your toilet paper supply. Put out fresh towels.

There are two keys to all of this: 1) Let the cleaner sit long enough to loosen up the dirt and disinfect the surface. 2) Clean the bathroom every week. Pick a day that is your bathroom cleaning day and just do it. When you keep up on your cleaning it doesn't become such an insurmountable project.

Garden Cleaning

Whether in the garden, yard or in the house, all of us have, at one time or another, had to deal with pests. Following are some ways to get rid of insects and other pests without spending a lot on expensive products.

1. For garden pests, make a mixture of 1 tablespoon liquid dishwashing soap and 1 cup of cooking oil. Mix about 3 tablespoons of this concentrate with a quart of water in a pump bottle and spray on plants.
2. Sprinkle cayenne pepper around plants to keep cats away.
3. Cucumber peel on a kitchen shelf will deter ants. You can also try washing or spraying your cabinets with vinegar and water.
4. Basil is a natural insect repellent. Keep a pot in your kitchen. Take a few leaves along with you on a picnic and put them out on the table to keep the flies away.
5. Bay leaves in your pantry will keep pests away. A bay leaf in a container of flour, cornmeal, or cereal will keep weevils out.
6. Plant peppermint around your house. It will keep ants out and it repels mice also.
7. Also cinnamon sprinkled around your foundation is said to keep ants out.

8. Weeds are not really pests, but they can be really pesky! Hot water will kill most unwanted plants—just boil some water and pour it over the plant you want to kill. Some weeds may require more than one dousing!
9. Mint tea bags can be used in your clothing drawers or in your closet to repel moths.

Whatever routine you use when you clean, using these hints for natural cleaning products can save you money. Other advantages are: no extra packaging to dispose of and fewer toxic chemicals in your home.

1. To clean windows and mirrors, mix equal parts of vinegar and water in a spray bottle. Spray on windows and wipe off with crumpled up newspapers.
2. To remove stains from carpet and upholstered furniture, mix equal parts of white vinegar, liquid dish detergent and water. Spray on stains and scrub with a brush and rinse with water. Another trick is to use shaving cream to clean carpet stains. Just scrub it in and rinse and let dry.
3. For a natural carpet deodorizer, sprinkle carpet with baking soda. Let sit for a few minutes; then vacuum as usual.
4. Mix equal parts olive oil and lemon juice for a natural furniture polish. Just apply with a soft cloth and buff to a shine. You can also use this on wood panelling.
5. When you have cleaned out your kitchen drawers, a bay leaf placed in the bottom will discourage bugs.
6. For a general all-purpose cleaner (instead of cleaners like Fantastik, etc.) mix 2 teaspoons each of borax and baking soda in 1 quart water. Put in a spray bottle.
7. Put an old sock on your hand, dampen it a little, and dust the leaves of your houseplants. Add a dab of mayonnaise and your plants' leaves will shine!

8. To clean the toilet, sprinkle in baking soda and scrub with a brush.
9. If you have rust stains in your bathtub or sink, pour on hydrogen peroxide and sprinkle on a little cream of tartar. Let it sit for a half hour or so, then wipe clean.
10. For cleaning bathroom tile and fixtures, mix 1/2 cup vinegar with 2 cups rubbing alcohol and about 1 tablespoon of liquid dishwashing soap. Add this to a gallon of water.
11. Pour a cup of baking soda and a cup of vinegar down your drain followed by a quart of boiling water, to deodorize it and keep it flowing freely.

By using ordinary household products to clean, you can save money and at the same time do something positive for our environment.

Infection Control in Hotels

Housekeeping practices, if performed correctly through educational presentations, will create an area suitable for guests, visitor and healthcare worker to enter and be comfortable within the confines of the environment. The proper maintenance of a health care facility increases the awareness of other employees of the necessity of good sanitary practices. Good housekeeping practices increase moral and public relations. No one wants to work in an area that smells or is dirty.

Sanitation depends upon cleaning thoroughness. There should be procedures in writing to fit each area of the facility such as walls, floors, windows, beds, furniture, draperies, carpets, waste containers, bathrooms, equipment, stairs, elevators, special-care equipment and handling of infectious waste for disposal.

Guest Rooms

— All horizontal surfaces should be cleaned daily.

— Uncarpeted floors should be cleaned daily.

— Carpeted floors should be vacuumed daily or as needed according to manufacturer's recommendations. Procedures should be spelled out concerning disinfecting carpets that contain blood. The vacuum cleaner should be one that does not add airborne organisms to the environment. Change filters as needed.

— Bathroom should be cleaned daily or as needed. Remember that this area of the guests' room may contain high concentrations of body fluids that may neutralize the disinfectant being used.

— Sanitary procedures should beperformed with common sense in mind.

— Drapes should be examined for body fluids or soiling. They do not have to be removed from isolation rooms once the guest has either recovered or been placed in a different locale unless body soils are visible.

— Walls should be only spot cleaned. There is absolutely no need in washing walls after a guest has been dismissed from a room intended for any type of isolation.

— Normal disinfection procedures should be employed in cleaning rooms used for isolation.

— Stainless steel double-bucket system should be used in all areas of the facility. Plastic buckets tend to become soiled and difficult to clean.

— All waste paper baskets should be lined with a plastic bag.

— Housekeeping personnel should report to the executive housekeepers any equipment that is not functioning correctly.

Other Areas

— Entrances, lobbies, waiting rooms, hallways should be cleaned on a regular schedule or as needed depending on traffic.

— A disinfectant solutions is not really needed in these areas.

— Clean carpets according to manufacturer's recommendations. Make certain that you have discussed with the manufacturer that if blood is spilled on these carpets, what type of chemicals can be used without damaging the fabric. Remember that you must use a tuberculocidal disinfectant on blood spills.

— Examine walls for soilage. Spot clean any wall that contains soil.

Personnel

— Personnel should be free of skin lesions such as herpes, boils, etc.

— All employees in housekeeping should be educated on what requires work restriction due to illness.

— All housekeeping personnel should be ideally vaccinated against tetanus, hepatitis B and influenza. The chickenpox vaccine is now available for those without prior history of exposure or immunity.

— Rubella and measles vaccine should be part of the employee's responsibility prior to employment.

Regulated Trash

— All housekeeping personnel should be cognizant on what types of waste require regulation.

— All housekeeping personnel should have inservice education on Standard Precautions on a yearly basis.

Documentation of such education should be made available to any licensing agency.

Summation

— Housekeeping is responsible for selecting a disinfectant, writing procedures on how to dilute it and when it should be changed during usage.

— Housekeeping personnel need yearly inservices on infection control practices.

— Cleaning in wrong sequences may increase the chance of microbial contamination.

— Use of dry-dusting increases aerosols.

— Use of reusable rather than disposable gloves affords the housekeeper more protection.

— Never store mops in a wet condition. This will increase proliferation of organisms. They should be dried after cleaning.

— Make certain that housekeepers understand how to pickup sharps from the floor, i.e., needles.

— Housekeepers must be provided the appropriate barrier protection for their tasks, instructions on where they are located, how to take them off and where to place them after removal.

— All filters in rooms should be checked on a regular schedule. When a filter is removed (changed) from a particular area, the date of newly installed filter should be written clearly on its side with a marking pen. This will enable the housekeeper to determine how often these filters should be changed.

— Change curtains as needed.

— Clean blinds as needed.

— It is not necessary to discard toilet paper or paper towels following guest discharge regardless of the sickness unless they are visibly soiled with body fluids.

— Always make certain that paper towel dispensers are full and that soap dispensers are functional.

— Always check needle disposal boxes to make certain that they are not more than 3/4 full.

— Check to make certain that all screens are functioning correctly.

— Check schedules of waste pickup to make certain that excessive accumulation does not exist.

Techniques of Speedy Cleaning

Speed cleaning usually entails cleaning your entire hotelall in one day. For many people this does not work due to busy schedules. Should this be your case, dust your home one day, tackle the bathrooms the next etc. Whichever job you do complete the entire task. Dust the entire house or clean all the bathrooms. It takes time to pull out your cleaning equipment so keep going until you finish.

Divide and conquer. Many people become overwhelmed at the thought of cleaning their entire home at one time. A professional breaks a home into sections cleaning one section then moving to the next. Here is a basic outline to follow. Adjust the sections according to the layout of your home.

— Section one: Bedroom area and hallway

— Section two: Kitchen, dining area, den or family room

— Section three: Formal living room and dining room

— Section four: Laundry room and any remote rooms.

Also remember you may not need to clean formal living rooms or dining rooms each time you clean. Use that time to dust cobwebs, clean cabinets, windows etc. Deciding where to begin and how to proceed baffles many people.

Clean the top floor first beginning at the back working your way either down the steps or to the center if you are on the first floor. Following this pattern keeps you from dragging equipment and dirt over freshly vacuumed carpets. Once you have developed a cleaning routine stick with it. The more familiar you are with the flow the faster you clean.

Here is a common cleaning pattern to follow. Remember you will need to make adjustments based on the layout of your home. Empty the trash as you clean. You will be amazed at the amount of clutter that heads to the garbage when a trash bag is handy. Carry a second trash bag for items that can be taken to Goodwill.

1. Master bathroom
2. Hall bathroom
3. Dust all bedrooms, stairway railings and wall hangings
4. Vacuum the master bedroom, bedrooms, hallways then stairs
5. Clean kitchen
6. Dust family room and dining area
7. Vacuum or dust the floors in kitchen and family room and mop the kitchen floor
8. Half bathroom
9. Dust formal living room and dining room
10. Vacuum these areas and damp mop the entry way if it has hard flooring.
11. Laundry rooms and any remote rooms like guest rooms or offices

People often follow a different procedure each time they clean a room and each room they clean. The secret to speed cleaning lies in repetition. Begin either at the left or the right of the room depending on which feels more comfortable to you. Then circle the room.

Bathrooms:

1. Spray the inside of the toilet with the bowl cleaner.
2. Spray the rim, toilet seat, counter top and sink with your all-purpose cleaner. Remember each time you put a bottle down and pick it up, you waste time.
3. Use your diluted orange cleaner and squirt down the shower or tub enclosure.
4. Next clean the toilet and toilet rim by sprinkling baking soda or Bar Keepers Friend on your toilet bowl brush.
5. Spray only the part of the mirror that is dirty wiping it down with a clean rag. That puts enough cleaner on the towel to clean the rest of the mirror.
6. Wipe the counter, sink and the exterior of the toilet and the floor behind.
7. Next clean the shower walls. Spray the shower floor and clean it. Finish by mopping the floor.

Dusting:

1. Lift objects with one hand then dust with the other. Place an old clean cotton tube sock over your dusting hand and lightly dampen it with your cleaner. People with arthritis or hand dexterity problems find it helpful to wear a rubber glove on one hand giving them a better grasp on objects.
2. Spray a lint free towel with the window cleaning solution and toss that over one shoulder to clean any glass inlaid tables or cabinets.
3. Begin dusting from either the right or the left and work your way around the room dusting window sills and wall hangings as you come to them.

4. For homes with pets, tuck a clean pair of rubber gloves into your back pocket. When you come to couches or chairs with pet hair, use the gloves and work your hands in a circular motion moving over the furniture. Toss the rolled up lint onto the floor for the vacuum to pick up. Some people cover furniture with a body size bath towel to keep them clean from pet hair. Easy to launder, towels also save on furniture wear and tear.
5. As you dust move furniture towards the center of the room to vacuum behind it.

Kitchens

1. Place a coffee cup half full of water in the microwave. Cook on high for two minutes. The resulting steam loosens any baked on food for easy cleaning. Allow the cup to cool for a minute before moving it so you don't scald yourself.
2. Spray the stove or any counter area that contains dried food with Bio Ox.
3. Start at the left and work your way clockwise around the kitchen leaving the sink for last after you mop the floor.
4. Move appliances to one side then spray the counter, dishwasher, refrigerator or microwave if it is in that immediate area.
5. Clean one section of cabinets each time you clean the kitchen, paying special attention to door pulls.
6. Mop the floor using a 100% terry cloth towel. Rinsing mops and filling buckets of water consumes time. A towel rinses quickly under a faucet then can be laundered for easy care.
7. Sprinkle the sink with Bar Keepers Friend or baking soda using a brush to thoroughly scrub the sink.

Vacuum: Vacuum around the room in the same order you dust. Vacuum behind furniture first, replace the furniture then back out of the room. If the floors are hard wood or laminated wood, dust them then damp mop using terry towel dampened with a small amount of white vinegar and water. For all other hard surface floors, vacuum them then damp mop using hot water only. Marble floors must be dried.

Hotel Cleaning Checklist

To generate a checklist for your hotel cleaning process is not a tough job. Make it once and you will have the benefit of minimizing your precious time, while you think for the arrangements to be made for your hotel cleaning. Making a checklist for hotel cleaning purpose is to give you knowledge about 'How much time will be consumed?',' How tiresome it will be','how good it will be' and so on. When you are going to make the checklist for the first time, better make a list of the tasks, which consumes major time in doing the task. For example, laundries, soaking the curtains are few to say. Make sure you have listed the tasks in store for you. Read further to know about few general checklist issues for cleaning your hotel.

— *Where To Begin Hotel Cleaning*. Start with the bathroom first. The most awful place of your hotel, your bathroom is the first place to clean. Then move on to the kitchen. This is the second irksome place that needs the cleaning then and there. As soon as you cleanup these two places, you will feel relieved as if you have done much of the entire cleaning process. Then go for the laundry task and then for cleaning the floors and so on.

— *Take Time Off Between Cleaning*. Cleaning process of your hotel is not something fun to most people. This extra effort to keep your hotel finicky and hygienic can actually be kept light by making time to take coffee, watching TV or listening to some good music in between the schedule.

— *Open Up The Windows During And After Cleaning.* As we use lot of chemical based cleansers, it's important to keep all the windows open for some time to let a fresh air inside the hotel. This will help you, stay away from getting infected with these harsh cleansers.

6

Laundry Operations

Laundry was probably first done in streams and letting the stream carry away the materials causing stains and smells. Laundry may still be done this way in some less industrialized areas and rural regions. Agitation helps remove the dirt, so the laundry is often rubbed, twisted, or slapped against flat rocks. Wooden bats or clubs could be used to help with beating the dirt out. These were called washing beetles.

Various chemicals may be used increase the solvent power of water, such as the compounds in soaproot or yucca-root used by Native American tribes. Soap, a compound made from lye and fat, is an ancient and very common laundry aid. However, modern washing machines typically use powdered or liquid laundry detergent in place of soap.

When no streams were available, laundry was done in water-tight vats or vessels. Sometimes large metal cauldrons were filled with fresh water and heated over a fire; boiling water was even more effective than cold in removing dirt. The washboard, a corrugated slab of a hard material such as metal, replaced rocks as a surface for loosening soil. Once clean, the clothes were wrung out — twisted to remove most of the water. Then they were hung up on poles or clotheslines to dry, or sometimes just spread out on clean grass.

The industrial revolution completely transformed laundry technology. First came the mangle, in the 18th century — two long rollers in a frame and a crank to revolve them. A laundry-worker took sopping wet clothing and cranked it through the mangle, compressing the cloth and expelling the excess water. The mangle was much quicker than hand twisting.

In the early 20th century inventors further mechanized the laundry process with various washing machines. Typically, these machines used an electrically powered agitator to replace tedious hand rubbing against a washboard. The earliest machines were simply a tub on legs, with a hand-operated mangle on top. Later the mangle too was electrically powered, then replaced by a perforated double tub, which spun out the excess water in a spin cycle. Laundry drying was also mechanized, with clothes dryers. Dryers were also spinning perforated tubs, but they blew heated air rather than water.

Washing machines and dryers are now fixtures in homes around the world. In some parts of the world, such as the USA and Switzerland, apartment buildings and dormitories often have laundry rooms, where residents share washing machines and dryers. Usually the machines are set to run only when coins in appropriate amounts are inserted in a coin slot. Those without home machines or access to laundry rooms must either wash their clothes by hand or visit a commercial laundromat.

In parts of Europe, apartment buildings with laundry rooms are uncommon, and each apartment has its own washing machine. All washing machines work by using mechanical energy, thermal energy, and chemical action.

Mechanical energy is imparted to the clothes load by the rotation of the agitator in top loaders, or by the tumbling action of the drum in front loaders. Thermal energy is supplied by the temperature of the wash bath.

Clothing has been hand-washed for thousands of years, by flushing water through the fabric to remove loose dirt, rubbing with soap to remove oils and stains, and applying fragrances to cover odors. For particularly dirty clothing caked with mud or dirt, it was necessary to constantly rub and flex the cloth to break apart solids and help the soap penetrate through thick, dry, or sticky layers of soil on the cloth. At first this was done by pounding or rubbing the clothing with rocks in a river, and later developed into the corrugated wash board. In Roman times a fuller would whiten clothing by stomping on it in a bucket full of fermented urine.

Washing machine technology was initially developed as a way to reduce the physical drudgery of this laborious scrubbing and rubbing process, by providing an open basin or sealed container with paddles or fingers to automatically agitate the clothing. The earliest machines were often hand-operated but were built with the belief that the machine itself was faster and easier to operate than washing the clothing by hand directly. Because electricity was not commonly available until at least 1930, these early machines were often operated by a low-speed single-cylinder hit and miss gasoline engine.

Because water usually had to be heated on a fire for washing, the warm soapy water was precious and would be reused over and over, first to wash the least soiled clothing, then to wash progressively dirtier clothing. The load of soaking wet clothing would be removed, and another load of dirty clothes added to the machine. While the earliest machines were constructed entirely from wood, later machines made of metal permitted a fire to burn below the washtub, to keep the water warm throughout the day's washing.

Removal of soap and water from the clothing after washing was originally a separate process. The soaking wet clothing would be formed into a roll and twisted by hand to extract water. To help reduce this labor, the wringer/mangle was developed, which uses two rollers under spring tension to sqeeze water out of the clothing. Each piece of clothing would be fed through the wringer separately. The first wringers were hand-operated, but were eventually included as a powered attachment above the washer tub. The wringer would be swung over the wash tub so that extracted wash water would fall back into the tub to be reused for the next wash load.

The modern process of water removal by spinning did not come into use until electric motors were developed. Spinning requires a constant high-speed power source, and was originally done in a separate device known as an extractor. A load of washed clothing would be transferred from the wash tub to the extractor basket, and the water spun out. These early extractors were often dangerous to use since unevenly distributed loads would cause the machine to shake violently. Many efforts have been made to counteract the shaking of unstable loads, first by mounting the spinning basket on a free-floating shock-absorbing frame to absorb minor imbalances, and a bump switch to detect severe movement and stop the machine so that the load can be manually redistributed. Many modern machines are equipped with a sealed ring of liquid around the top of the basket that works to counteract any imbalances.

What is now commonly referred to as an automatic washer was at one time referred to as a washer/extractor, which combines the features of these two separate devices into a single machine, plus also includes the ability to fill and drain water by itself. It is possible to take this a step further, to also merge the automatic washing machine and clothes dryer into a single device, but this is generally uncommon because the drying process tends to use much more energy than using two separate devices; a combined washer/dryer not only must dry the clothing, but also needs to dry out the wash chamber itself.

Traditional Laundry Practices

Large hotels could employ a maids specifically to deal with the washing, but smaller hoteliers had to fend for themselves or employ the services of a laundress. Sometimes these would be women who would come into the house to do the washing, rather like a maid, but more often they took washing to their own homes.

A laundress doing her work

The work could be very skilled and laundresses could make quite a healthy income. However, it was always arduous. The women would work six days a week and in many cases would do the work for the whole of their lives.

Washing day was a major event in the Victorian household. Due to the labour involved, it was also infrequent, occurring perhaps once a month to be more economically viable. The less frequent the washing, the more affluent a family could claim to be, as they would have sufficient clothing to wear until next wash day.

Large country houses would have a purpose-built laundry, an idea which was copied by larger homes and farmhouses. Smaller homes had to content themselves with using the kitchen or the yard for the purpose. Before indoor plumbing, water often had to be carried some distance. Efforts were made to store rainwater, and rural communities could still use streams for washing.

The use of soap for washing increased throughout the second half of the nineteenth century after the tax on it was abolished in 1853. Over a stone (16lbs) of soap per person was being used by 1891. In addition, sometimes bleaches and 'blue' were used for white clothes. Starch was used for linens, aprons and collars and this was often regarded as a specialist skill.

Washing was done in tubs or bucks. These were usually wooden, although metal ones were becoming more common. The actual washing was done with a 'dolly' - a pole with one end shaped either like a cone or a small three-legged stool. This was used to plunge and agitate the clothes in the boiling water. Washboards were becoming more popular, used with a wider, bath shaped tub; these were easier and quicker to use than the old dollies. Clothes would be rubbed with soap to remove stains. Washing machines, although in existence in 1891, were not generally popular and were expensive to buy and run.

Dolly tub and peg

The process of washing lasted for most of the day and had to be started early in order to get it all dried. It was still quite usual to dry washing on hedges or even on mown fields, or on clothes horses and lines in the house in wet weather.

'Vowel' washing machine

When the items were fully washed and rinsed, they would be wrung to remove excess water, and hung to dry. Once dry or nearly dry, clothes and bedding would be mangled to smoothe them, sometimes taking the place of ironing. Mangles might also be used for wringing clothes. Mangles were widely owned as they became smaller and more affordable.

Drying rail

Finally the items would be ironed. Flat irons were of various weights but did not keep their heat for long periods. Irons came in various types and sizes, for different fuels and ironing tasks

Tools of Laundry

Laundry Detergent

Laundry detergents come in all shapes and scents these days. Be sure that you find one that fits the needs of your family and your machine. Skin sensitivities, machine manuals, and scent preferences will probably make a big difference in which brand you ultimately buy, but the majority of brands on the market do a fantastic job at washing your clothing.

Stain removers

No matter how careful we are, stains happen. What's worse, is that they make no distinction between nice clothes and play clothes. Everything is subject to stains. When stains happen, it's important to use the right stain remover or removal method to protect your clothing. Be sure to read the directions on your stain remover to know if the garment will need to be washed right away.

Bleach

Up until recently there wasn't much choice for a consumer looking for bleach. All brands were relatively alike. No, however, there are scented bleaches, and even new thicker formulas designed to not spill or splash as much. There are even formulas that can be poured directly on bleachable fabrics. In addition to these chlorine bleach achievements, there are many colorsafe bleaches on the market for consumers to choose from. These bleaches work to remove stains, while still brightening colors.

Other laundry additives

There are many laundry additives on the market. They range from brighteners, to whiteners. Fabric softener, dryer sheets, boosters, and water softeners are just a few of the products you'll find waiting in the laundry aisle. If you have a laundry problem, chances are, there's an additive that can help. Be sure to read directions carefully on additives, and test for colorfastness in a hidden spot to be sure it's going to achieve the results you want.

Laundry Sink or Bucket

Having a sink close in or near your laundry room is wonderful. It gives you the ability to treat stains, clean up spills, and clean the laundry room much more easily. If you don't have a laundry sink, investing in a new large bucket might be a great idea. This laundry bucket is handy for time when stained items might need to soak.

Drying Rack

Chances are you have a few items in your closet that require special drying care. You may not have realized it when you bought them, but one trip through the dryer will turn them into clothes that even a fashion doll would have a hard time fitting into. A collapsible drying rack can hide out of sight until you need it.

Hampers and baskets

Hampers and baskets are necessary for storing, sorting,

and carrying loads of laundry. The number of hampers and baskets you will need will depend on the makeup of your household. Some people prefer to have a hamper in each bedroom and family bathroom. Others prefer simple laundry baskets in these rooms, with hampers located in the laundry room. Decide how you need these items to be setup to best help your family.

Hampers

Washer and Dryer

Today's washers and dryers are amazingly efficient and effective at cleaning our clothing while protecting it. The newest features on these machines seem to change every month, and while we don't yet have a machine that will retrieve, sort, wash, dry, iron, fold, and put away without any human contact, we can all hope that we're getting closer to developing such a dream machine.

Washing machine

The first English patent under the category of Washing and Wringing Machines was issued in 1691. A drawing of an early washing machine appeared in the January 1752 issue of "The Gentlemen's Magazine," an English publication. In 1782 Henry Sidgier was issued a British patent for a rotating drum washer.

Washing machine

The first United States Patent titled "Clothes Washing" was granted to Nathaniel Briggs of New Hampshire in 1797. Fire destroyed the patent office and no description of the device exists so it is not known what kind of washing device Briggs "invented."

The electric washing machine was first mass produced in 1906. It is not known who first invented the electric washer. Alva J. Fisher has been incorrectly credited with the invention of the electric washer.

Although somewhat cyclic, US electric washing machine sales increased after World War I, reaching 913,000 units in 1928. The main reason why so many people bought the washing machine was because it saved people lots of time in domestic tasks, and the result was that society's expectations for cleanliness went up. However, high unemployment in the Depression years hit sales; by 1932 the number of units shipped was down to about 600,000.

The first laundromat opened in Fort Worth, Texas in 1934. It was run by a man under the name Andrew Clein. Patrons used coin-in-the-slot facilities to rent washing machines. Since then, laundromats have become common.

Washer design improved markedly during the 1930s; the mechanism was now enclosed within a cabinet; more attention was paid to electrical safety; spin dryers were introduced, to replace the dangerous power wringers of the day.

Early automatic washing machines were usually connected to the water supply via temporary slip-on connectors to the sink taps. Later, permanent connections to both the hot and cold water supplies became the norm. Most modern front-loading European machines now only have a cold water connection and rely completely on electric heaters to raise the water temperature.

By 1940, 60% of the 25,000,000 wired homes in the United States had an electric washing machine. Many of these machines featured a power wringer, although built-in spin dryers were not uncommon.

Bendix introduced the first automatic washing machine in 1937, having applied for a patent in the same year.In appearance and mechanical detail, this first machine is not unlike the front loading automatic washers produced today. Although it included many of the today's basic features, the machine lacked any drum suspension and therefore had to be anchored to the floor to prevent "walking".

Many of these early automatic machines had coin-in-the-slot facilities and were installed in the basement laundry rooms of apartment houses. Naturally, after the attack on Pearl Harbor, US domestic washer production had to be suspended for the duration of World War II. However, many US appliance manufacturers were given permission to undertake the research and development of washers during the war years. Many took the opportunity to develop automatic machines, realising that these represented the future for the industry.

General Electric introduced the first top loading automatic also in 1947. This machine had many of the features that are incorporated into modern machines.

A large number of US manufacturers introduced competing automatic machines (mainly of the top loading type) in the late 1940s/early 1950s. Several manufacturers even produced semi-automatic machines, where the user had to intervene at one or two points in the wash cycle.

Since their introduction in the late 1930s/mid 1940s, automatic washing machines have relied on mechanical timers to sequence the washing and extraction process. Mechanical timers consist of a series of cams on a common shaft. At the appropriate time in the wash cycle, each cam actuates a switch to engage/disengage a particular part of the machinery. The timer shaft is driven by a small electric motor via a reduction gearbox.

On the early mechanical timers the motor ran at a constant speed throughout the wash cycle, although it was possible for the user to truncate parts of the program, by manually advancing the control dial. However, by the 50s demand for greater flexibility in the wash cycle led to the introduction of electronic timers to supplement the basic mechanical timer. These electronic timers enable greater variation in such functions as the wash time. With this arrangement, the electric timer motor is periodically switched-off to permit the clothing to soak, and is only re-energised just prior to a micro-switch being engaged/ disengaged.

Despite the high cost of automatic washers, manufacturers had difficulty in meeting the pent-up demand. Although there were material shortages during the Korean War, by 1953 automatic washing machine sales in the US exceeded those of wringer-type electric machines.

In the UK, electric washing machines did not become popular until the 1950s. The early electric washers were single tub, wringer-type machines, automatic washing machines being extremely expensive. During the 1960s, twin tub machines briefly became very popular, helped by the low price of the Rolls Razor washers. Automatic washing machines did not really become common in the UK until well into the 1970s.

In early automatic washing machines, any changes in impeller/drum speed were achieved by mechanical means or by a rheostat on the motor power supply. However, since the 1970s electronic control of motor speed has become a common feature on the more expensive models.

Early front loading machines, especially those manufactured in Mediterranean countries (e.g. Italy), had relatively low spin speeds (e.g. 800rpm or less). Nowadays, a spin speed of 1200rpm is common and a peak spin speed as high as 1600rpm is available on some machines. However, because they were not susceptible to gravitational forces, some early top loading machines had spin speeds in excess of 1000rpm, although some were as low as 360rpm.

In the late 1990s, the British inventor James Dyson launched a type of washing machine with two cylinders rotating in opposite directions; which, it is claimed, reduces the wash time and produces cleaner results; however, this machine is not currently in production.

In the 1990s upmarket machines incorporated microcontrollers for the timing process. These proved reliable, so many cheaper machines now incorporate microcontrollers, rather than mechanical timers. Washing machines are a classic application for fuzzy logic.

Modern washing machines are available in two main configurations: top loading and front loading. The top loading design, most popular in the United States, Canada, Australia and some parts of Europe, places the clothes in a vertically-mounted perforated basket that is contained within a water-retaining tub, with a propeller-like agitator in the center of the bottom of the basket. Clothes are loaded through the top of the machine, which is covered with a hinged door. During the wash cycle, the outer tub is filled with water sufficient to suspend the clothing freely in the basket, and the movement of the agitator pulls the clothing downward in the center towards the agitator paddles. The clothing then moves outward and up the sides of the basket to repeat the process. Top-loaders are not well-suited to cleaning large objects such as pillows or sleeping bags due to the tendency for them to just float on the surface of the water without circulating, and the aggressive agitator action can damage delicate fabrics.

In most top loading washers, if the motor spins in one direction, the gearbox drives the agitator; if the motor spins the other way, the gearbox locks the agitator and spins the basket and agitator together. Similarly if the pump motor rotates one way it recirculates the sudsy water; in the other direction it pumps water from the machine during the spin cycle. Because they usually incorporate a gearbox, clutch, crank, etc, top loading washers are mechanically more complex than front loading machines but are generally lower maintenance since there is no need for a complex door seal.

The front loading design, most popular in Europe and the Middle East, mounts the inner basket and outer tub horizontally, and loading is through a glass door at the front of the machine. Agitation is supplied by the back-and-forth rotation of the cylinder and by gravity. The clothes are lifted up by paddles on the inside wall of the drum and then dropped. This motion flexes the weave of the fabric and forces water and detergent solution through the clothes load. Because the wash action does not require the clothing be freely suspended in water, only enough water is needed to moisten the fabric. Because less water is required, front-loaders typically use less soap, and the aggressive dropping and folding action of the tumbling can easily produce large amounts of foam.

Front-loaders control water usage through the surface tension of water, and the capillary wicking action this creates in the fabric weave. A front-loader washer always fills to the same low water level, but a large pile of dry clothing standing in water will soak up the moisture, causing the water level to drop. The washer then refills to maintain the original water level. Because it takes time for this water absorption to occur with a motionless pile of fabric, nearly all front-loaders begin the washing process by slowly tumbling the clothing under the stream of water entering and filling the drum, to rapidly saturate the dry cloth with water.

Front loading washers are mechanically relatively simple compared to top-loaders, with the main motor normally being connected to the drum via a grooved pulley belt and large pulley wheel, without the need for a gearbox, clutch or crank. But front-load washers suffer from their own technical problems, due to the drum lying sideways. For example, a top loading washer keeps water inside the tub merely through the force of gravity pulling down on the water, while a front-loader must tightly seal the door shut with a gasket to prevent dripping water onto the floor during the wash cycle. This access door is locked shut during the entire wash cycle, since opening the door with the machine in use could result in water gushing out onto the floor. For front-loaders without viewing windows on the door, it is possible to accidentally pinch fabric between the door and the drum, resulting in tearing and damage to the pinched clothing during tumbling and spinning.

Nearly all front-loader washers for the consumer market must also use a folded flexible bellows assembly around the door opening, to keep clothing contained inside the basket during the tumbling wash cycle. If this bellows assembly were not used, small articles of clothing such as socks could slip out of the wash basket near the door, and fall down the narrow slot between the outer tub and basket, plugging the drain and possibly jamming rotation of the inner basket. Retrieving lost items from between the outer tub and inner basket can require complete disassembly of the front of the washer and pulling out the entire inner wash basket. Commercial and industrial front-loaders used by businesses usually do not use the bellows, and instead require all small objects to be placed in a mesh bag to prevent loss near the basket opening.

This bellows assembly around the door is the source of problems for the consumer front-loader. The bellows has a large number of flexible folds to permit the tub to move separately from the door during the high speed extraction cycle. These folds can collect lint, dirt, and moisture, resulting in mold and mildew growth and a foul odor. Some front-loading washer operating instructions say the bellows should be wiped down monthly with a strong bleach solution, while others offer a special freshening cycle where the machine is run empty with a strong dosing of bleach.

A top-loading washer suffers from none of these continued maintenance problems and needs no regular freshening. During the spin cycle, a top-loading tub is free to move about inside the cabinet of the machine, using only a lip around the top of the inner basket and outer tub to keep the spinning water and clothing from spraying out over the edge.

There are many variations of these two general themes. Top loading machines in Asia use impellers instead of agitators. Impellers are similar to agitators except that they do not have the center post extending up in the middle of the wash tub basket. There is also a variant of the horizontal axis design that is designed by Staber Industries that is loaded from the top, through a small door in the circumference of the drum. These machines usually have a shorter cylinder and are therefore smaller, but offer the efficiency of a front-loader while eliminating the problems of the flexible bellows.

Front-loaded machines are ideal for fitted/finished kitchens, since they can be installed under a countertop/ worktop. A front loading washing machine, in a fully-fitted kitchen, is often disguised as an ordinary base cabinet/unit. They are also ideal for small homes and apartments with limited space, because the dryer can be installed directly above the washer.

Many front loading machines have electrical heating elements to heat the wash bath to near boiling, if desired. Chemical action is supplied by the detergent and other laundry chemicals. Front loaders use special detergents that are designed to release different chemical ingredients at different temperatures. This is so that different type of stains and soils will be cleaned from the clothes as the wash water is heated up by the electrical heater. Front loaders also need to use low sudsing detergents because the tumbling action of the drum folds air into the clothes load that can cause over sudsing.

Tests comparing front loading and top loading machines have shown that, in general, front-loaders wash clothes more thoroughly, cause less wear, and use less water and energy than top-loaders. As a result of using less water, they require less detergent to be used, or conversely, they can use the same amount of detergent with less water, which increases detergent concentration and increases the amount of chemical action. They also allow a dryer to be more easily mounted directly above the washer.

Top-loaders have the advantage that they complete a washing cycle much faster and allow clothes to be removed at intermediate stages of the cycle (for instance, if some clothes within a wash are not to be spun). They also tend to be easier to load and unload, since reaching into the tub does not require stooping. The top loader's spin cycle between washing and rinsing allows an extremely simple fabric softener dispenser, which operates passively through centrifugal force and gravity. The same objective must be accomplished by a solenoid-operated valve on a front loader. Another advantage to the top loading design is the reliance on gravity to contain the water, rather than potentially trouble-prone or short-lived front door seals.

Traditionally, top loading machines have tended to be more complex mechanically than front loading washers, because the former generally require a gearbox, clutch, crank, etc to perform the wash cycle. However, the recent introduction of direct drive motors has greatly simplified some of the top loading washers on the market. Also, because of the introduction of electronics, modern machines are far less complex than the early automatic washers. Consequently, the price of automatic machines, in real terms, has fallen considerably.

Tunnel washer

A tunnel washer, also called a continuous batch washer, is a computerized industrial laundry machine designed specifically to handle heavy loads. As the name implies, the device consists of a long metal tube called a tunnel. A huge metal spiral called an archimedes screw runs down the center of the tunnel, dividing it into sections called "pockets". As the screw rotates, linen is forced from one end of the tunnel to the other. Since the screw is made of porous metal, laundry can move through the washer in one direction while water and chemicals are forced through in the other. Thus, the linen moves through pockets of progressively cleaner water and fresher chemicals. Soiled linen continuously goes into one end of the tunnel while clean linen moves continuously out of the other. Since their introduction in the late 1960s, tunnel washers have become progressively more reliable. Though extremely expensive, they are now common in major hotel, hospital and other high-volume laundry departments. From the start, one of the machine's major drawbacks was the necessity of using one wash formula for each item. Modern tunnel washers can monitor and adjust the chemical levels in individual pockets, effectively overcoming this problem.

Clothes dryer

A clothes dryer or tumble dryer is a household appliance that is used to remove the residual moisture from a load of clothing and other textiles, generally shortly after they are cleaned in a washing machine. Most dryers consist of a rotating drum called a tumbler through which heat is circulated to evaporate the moisture from the load. The tumbler is rotated relatively slowly in order to maintain space between the articles in the load. In most cases, the tumbler is belt-driven by an induction motor.

There are two general classes of rotating dryers: electric and gas. Both of these refer to the method used to raise the temperature of the air flowing through the tumbler, since the tumbling action is usually electrically powered.

The electric dryer generally uses a coiled wire that is heated with electric current. The amount of electric current is varied to adjust the air temperature. In the United States and other countries following USA wiring standards, electric dryers typically have a 4-wire NEMA 14-30 plug, rather than the 3-wire NEMA 5-15 plug used by most appliances, and need a 30-ampere, 240-volt centertapped single-phase circuit. Small "portable" clothes dryers, popular with urban dwellers, normally use conventional 110 volt connections. The gas dryer employs a gas burner that burns natural gas, propane, or butane to form a jet of hot gases that are directed into a venturi chamber, which uses Bernoulli's principle to pull in ambient air and raise its temperature. The air temperature can be altered by adjusting the size of the gas flame or, more commonly, by merely extinguishing it and relighting it. Gas dryers require electricity to spin the clothes, but the amount of electricity is much smaller than in an electric dryer removing the need for a special connection. The motors normally run on standard 110 volt electricity.

Traditional dryers

Traditional dryers continuously draw in the cool, dry, ambient air around them and heat it before passing it through the tumbler. Afterwards, the resulting hot, humid air is simply vented outside to make room for more dry air to continue the drying process. The traditional design makes no effort to recycle the heat put into the load, and so is quite inefficient. Nevertheless, the basic design is simple, reliable, and cheap.

Spin dryers

These machines simply spin their drums faster than a typical washer could in order to extract additional water from the load. They may remove more water in two minutes than a heated tumbler dryer can in twenty, thus saving significant amounts of time and energy. Although spinning alone will not completely dry clothing, this additional step saves a worthwhile amount of time and energy for large laundry operations such as those of hospitals or hotels.

Condensation dryers

Just as in a normal dryer, condensation dryers pass heated air through the load. However, instead of exhausting this air, the dryer uses a heat exchanger to cool the air and condense the water vapor into either a drain pipe or a collection tank. Afterwards, this air is run through the loop again. The heat exchanger uses ambient air as its coolant, therefore the heat produced by the dryer will go into the immediate surroundings instead of the outside.

Because the heat exchange process simply cools the Internal air using ambient air, it will not dry the air in the internal loop to as low a level of humidity as the fresh, ambient air. As a consequence of the increased humidity of the air used to dry the load as well as the increased complexity of the design, this type of dryer requires more time and energy than a traditional dryer. However, it is a valid option where long, intricate ducting would be required to vent a traditional dryer.

Heat pump dryers

Whereas condensation dryers use a passive heat exchanger cooled by ambient air, these dryers use a heat pump. The hot, humid air from the tumbler is passed through a heat pump where the cold side condenses the water vapor into either a drain pipe or a collection tank and the hot side reheats the air. In this way not only does the dryer avoid the need for ducting, but it also conserves much of its heat within the dryer instead of exhausting it into the surroundings. Heat pump dryers can therefore use less than half the energy required by either condensation or traditional dryers. As with condensation dryers, the heat exchanger will not dry the internal air to as low a level of humidity as the ambient air. With respect to ambient air, the higher humidity of the air used to dry the clothes has the effect of increasing drying times; however, because heat pump dryers conserve much of the heat of the air they use, the already-hot air can be cycled more quickly, possibly leading to shorter drying times than traditional dryers, depending on the model.

Mechanical steam compression dryers

A new type of dryer in development, these machines are a more advanced version of heat pump dryers. Instead of using hot air to dry the clothing, mechanical steam compression dryers use water recovered from the clothing in the form of steam. First, the tumbler and its contents are heated to 100 °C. The wet steam that results purges the system of air and is the only remaining atmosphere in the tumbler.

As wet steam exits the tumbler, it is mechanically compressed (hence the name) to extract water vapor and transfer the heat of vaporization to the remaining gaseous steam. This pressurized, gaseous steam is then allowed to expand and is superheated before being injected back into the tumbler where its heat causes more water to vaporize from the clothing, creating more wet steam and restarting the cycle.

Like heat pump dyers, mechanical steam compression dryers recycle much of the heat used to dry the clothes, and they operate in a very similar range of efficiency as heat pump dryers. Both types can be over twice as efficient as traditional dryers. However, the considerably higher temperatures used in mechanical steam compression dryers result in drying times on the order of half as long as those of heat pump dryers.

Dry cleaning

Dry cleaning is any cleaning process for clothing and textiles using an organic solvent other than water —

generally known as dry cleaning fluid, and typically this is tetrachloroethylene. Dry cleaning is necessary for cleaning items which would otherwise be damaged by water and soap or detergent. It may also be sought if washing by hand — another alternative for some delicate fabrics — is seen as laborious.

Dry cleaning uses non-water-based solvents to remove dirt and stains from clothes. The potential for using petroleum based solvents in this manner was first discovered in the mid-19th century by French dye-works owner Jean Baptiste Jolly, who noticed that his tablecloth became cleaner after his maid spilled kerosene on it, and from this observation developed a service to clean other people's clothes in this manner, which he termed "nettoyage à sec," or "dry cleaning" in English.

Early dry cleaners used petroleum-based solvents, such as gasoline and kerosene. Concerns over flammability led William Joseph Stoddard, a dry cleaner from Atlanta, to develop Stoddard solvent as a slightly less flammable alternative to gasoline-based solvents. The use of highly flammable petroleum solvents led to many fires and explosions, which resulted in heavy regulation of dry cleaners.

After World War I, dry cleaners began using various chlorinated solvents. These solvents were much less flammable than petroleum solvents and had much greater cleaning power. By the mid-1930s the dry cleaning industry had adopted tetrachloroethylene as a standard, colloquially called "perc," as the ideal solvent. It is stable, nonflammable, and has excellent cleaning power and is gentle to most garments.

A dry cleaning machine is somewhat similar to combination of a domestic washing machine, and clothes dryer. Garments are placed into a washing/extraction chamber. This is the core of the dry cleaning machine. The washing chamber contains a horizontal, perforated drum that rotates within an outer shell. The shell holds the solvent while the rotating drum holds the garment load. Depending on the size of the machine the basket capacity will be between 20 and 80 lb (9-36 kg) of garments.

During the wash cycle the chamber is filled approximately 1/3 full of solvent and begins to rotate to agitate the clothing. The solvent temperature is controlled at 85°F (29.4°C), as a higher temperature may extract dye from the garments, causing color loss. During the wash cycle, the chamber is constantly fed a supply of fresh solvent from the working solvent tank while spent solvent is removed and sent to a filter unit comprising a distillation boiler and condenser. The ideal flow rate is one gallon of solvent per pound of garments per minute, depending on the size of the machine.

Before being placed in the machine, garments are inspected for stains and soils by the operator. Depending on the nature of the soil, a catalyst may be applied to the soil; this depends on the operator's judgement of the makeup of the textile and the soil itself. Oil-based soils such as grease, oil or lipstick typically are removed very well by perchloroethylene, whereas water-based soils such as coffee, wine and perspiration will need a catalyst to allow the dry cleaning solvent to emulsify and lift them. Food based grease soils fall in between the two, and a milder catalyst may be applied.

Garments are also checked carefully for foreign objects; items such as plastic pens will dissolve in the solvent bath and may damage textiles beyond recovery. Some textile dyes are "loose" (red being the main culprit), and will shed dye during the solvent immersion; these will not be included in a load along with lighter-based coloured textiles to avoid colour transfer. In addition, the solvent used must be distilled to remove any impurities which may transfer to the clothes. Garments are checked carefully for dry cleaning textile compatibility, including the fasteners; many decorative fasteners are either not dry-cleaning-solvent proof, or will not withstand the mechanical action of the cleaning cycle. These will be removed and restiched after the cleaning, or protected with a small padded protector as needed. Finally, fragile items such as feather bedspreads or tasselled rugs or hangings may be enclosed into a loose mesh bag. The density of perchloroethylene is around 1.7 g/cm3 at room temperature, and the sheer weight of absorbed solvent may cause the textile to fail under normal force during the extraction cycle unless the mesh bag provides mechanical support.

A typical wash cycle lasts for 8-15 minutes depending on the type of garments and amount of soiling. During the first three minutes, solvent-soluble soils dissolve into the perchloroethylene and loose, insoluble soil from fabrics comes off. It takes approximately ten to twelve minutes after the loose soil has come off to remove all of the ground-in insoluble soil from the garments. Machines using hydrocarbon solvents require a much longer wash cycle of at least 25 minutes because of the much slower rate of solvation of solvent-soluble soils (e.g oily stains). A dry-cleaning surfactant "soap" may also be added.

At the end of wash cycle, the machine starts a rinse cycle and the garment load is rinsed with fresh distilled solvent from the pure solvent tank. This pure solvent rinse prevents discoloration of garments caused by soil particles being absorbed back onto the garment surface from the "dirty" working solvent.

After the rinse cycle the machine begins the extraction process. This process recovers dry cleaning solvent for reuse. Modern dry cleaning machines can recover approximately 99.99% of the solvent used in the cleaning process.

The extraction begins by draining the solvent out of the washing chamber cycle and accelerating the basket to speeds of 350 to 450 rpm, causing much of the solvent to spin free of the fabric. When no more solvent can be spun out, the machine starts its drying cycle.

During the drying cycle the garments are tumbled in continuous stream of warm air (145°F/63°C) that circulates through the basket evaporating any traces of solvent left behind after the spin cycle. The temperature of the air is carefully controlled to prevent over drying and heat damage to the garments. The warm air then passes through a chiller unit where the solvent vapors are condensed, and returned to the distilled solvent tank. Modern dry cleaning machines use a closed loop system where the chilled air is then reheated and recirculated. This results in very high solvent recovery rates.

After the drying cycle is completed, a deodorizing (aeration) cycle starts to cool the garments and remove the last traces of dry cleaning solvent, by circulating cool outside air over the garments and then through a vapor recovery filter made from activated carbon and polymer resins. At the end of the aeration cycle, the dry cleaned garments are clean and ready for pressing/finishing.

Working solvent from the washing chamber passes through several filtration steps before it is returned to the washing chamber. The first step is a button trap which prevents small objects (lint, fasteners, buttons, coins etc) from entering the solvent pump.

Next the solvent passes through a filter unit which removes lint and insoluble suspended soils from the solvent. Several different types are used, most filters use an ultra fine mesh to support a thin layer of filter powder (made from diatomaceous earth and activated clays). Some machines use powderless filters which are capable of removing soil particles greater than 30 micrometers from the solvent.

As the machine is used, a thin layer of filter cake (called muck) accumulates on the surface of the lint filter. The muck is removed regularly (once per day) and then further processed to recover any solvent trapped in the muck. Many machines use "spin disc filters" in which the muck is removed from the filter surface by centrifugal action while the filter is back-washed with solvent.

After passing through the lint filter, the solvent passes through an adsorptive cartridge filter. This filter is made from activated clays and charcoal and removes fine insoluble soil and non-volatile residues along with dyes from solvent. Finally the solvent passes through a polishing filter which removes any traces of soil not removed by the previous filters. The clean working solvent is then returned to the working solvent tank. To enhance cleaning power, small amounts of detergent (0.5%-1.5%) are added to the working solvent and are essential to its functionality. These detergents help dissolve hydrophilic soils and keep soil from redepositing on garments. Depending on the machine's design, either an anionic or cationic detergent is used.

Tips for Cleaning Clothes

Here are some effective tips for cleaning clothes.

1. Try to wait until you have a full load before running your washer or dryer.

2. The clothes dryer is one of the most energy hungry home appliances. To improve the energy efficiency of your dryer, frequently clean out the lint trap, and once or twice a year, unplug the dryer, remove the front lower panel, and vacuum out the cavity beneath the lint trap. It is amazing how much lint escapes from that trap into the dryer cavity. Not only does this lint buildup cause your dryer to need longer to dry clothes, it has also been known to cause fires.
3. Wash in cold water whenever possible. You do not need to wash with hot water unless you are trying to sterilise your laundry. Always set your rinse on the cold water setting. This saves the energy necessary to heat the water. Washing in cold water can save the typical family over $120 a year!
4. Plain white vinegar is a good substitute for fabric softener. Environmentally safe and nonallergenic, just add 1/2 to 3/4 cup as you would a liquid softener.
5. If you use softener sheets, a half sheet works as well as a whole one. Keep an empty tissue box near your dryer for used softener sheets; use these for dusting furniture.
6. Using 1/2 to 3/4 the recommended amount of laundry detergent will get clothes just as clean and leave less soap buildup.
7. Many garments labelled "Dry Clean Only" can be safely hand washed using mild soap like Woolite and cold water.
8. When washing dark clothes for the first time use cold water and put 1 tablespoon of salt in the water. The salt helps set the colour. To brighten dark clothes after they have been washed several times, repeat the procedure.

You can use lighter fluid on a variety of surfaces, first testing a less noticeable spot to make sure it won't do any damage. It's great on most floors, plastic, vinyl, some wood surfaces, basically anything you can dab it on and wipe off again. Lighter fluid will remove labels and adhesive from almost any surface. When we got our new refrigerator it had strapping tape stuck all over it. The lighter fluid took it right off. It removes crayon marks from most surfaces and also removes grease and oil stains. You can also use it to remove the black scuff marks on the rubber soles of your shoes, and to remove gum from most surfaces. Don't forget that lighter fluid is highly flammable and should be used with care. It is also inexpensive, easy to find, and you'll find so many uses for it you won't be able to live without it.

Organising your Clothes Closet

The clothes closet is often stuffed from floor to ceiling with clothing, briefcases, purses and shoes. Valuable clothing rod space has been taken over by vast armies of mismatched hangers. Books and magazines have managed to somehow sprout out of nowhere. Bed linens are mixed in with towels, umbrellas and shoes. You can barely see the floor. Before you know it, your closet has become clutter central! Following are some guidelines to organise your closet.

Get the proper supplies: Buy a starter set of 30 hangers, or 60 if the closet is shared by two people. Get the sturdy, plastic ones. They're inexpensive and can be obtained at a homegoods store. Buy all one colour for uniformity. While you're at the store, pick up a few sturdy skirt and pants hangers. Vertical skirt hangers with clips that hold 5 to 6 skirts on one hanger are a great choice. In addition, pick up an expandable shoe rack and a tie rack if you wear ties.

Start with a clean slate: Pull out everything that's currently in your closet. Keep in mind, as you're doing so, that you probably only wear 20% of your clothes on a regular basis, 10% of them are for special occasions, and the other 70% of them are probably never used at all.

Separate clothes into 5 piles:

a) Clothes that meet any of the following criteria:
   — it is outdated
   — it is ripped
   — it is stained
   — it doesn't fit
   — you think it may come back in fashion someday
   — you wouldn't dream of ever wearing it again

b) Wire hanger pile

c) Clothes that need minor repairs such as sewing a hem or replacing a button. If it's too much of a hassle to repair it, then don't put it in this pile.

d) Clothes you love and wear at least once a month and clothes you love and wear at least twice a year. Your wardrobe should always make you feel good about yourself. If you don't love it or wear it often, it doesn't belong in this pile.

e) Any other items that don't fit into category a, b, c or d.

Dump it or donate it: Grab a large plastic garbage bag and dump everything from your a pile into it. Bring it to your local charity organisation first thing in the morning or dump it now.

Repair it within 2 weeks: Now that your a and b piles are donated or trashed, let's move on to your c pile. This pile should contain those articles of clothing that need minor repair. Get a basket or container. Dump this entire pile in it. Now, carry that basket over to your clothing repair area.

Give yourself a 2 week deadline. If it's not done in two weeks, dump or donate the entire basket. After all, if it's not important enough for you to repair, it's clutter.

Organise your keepers: Sort everything in your d pile by category of clothing When done sorting, start with one category. Take one article of clothing at a time, put it on a hanger and hang it in the closet. Do this until you've managed to hang all of your categories of clothing, making sure that all clothing and hangers are facing the same direction.

Categorise and organise everything else: If, due to lack of additional storage space, you have some items that simply have to be returned to your closet which haven't been put there already, categorise them. Then, get some inexpensive organising containers so that each category remains separated and place the containers on shelves in your closet.

Finishing touches: Now, you're ready for some finishing touches. If you install a few hooks on an empty closet wall, you'll be able to hang belts, umbrellas and handbags. If you're lucky enough to have cubbies in your closet, purses and hats can be stored there; otherwise, put them on your closet shelves. You can even pick up a clear, over-the-door shoe bag for small accessories such as hosiery, scarves, jewelry and the like. Don't put shoes in the shoe bag. It may sound funny, but these bags are too flimsy and awkward for the weight of most shoes, plus they collect dirt from shoe bottoms.

Final thoughts: Don't overstuff. There should be plenty of room in your closet to get an item in or out. If there's not, consider thinning out your wardrobe a little more. The goal here is quality, not quantity. Don't buy another thing to wear without first determining if you really need it. Some people like to discard something they're not really happy with anymore, for a new item.

Stain Removal

Since plastic covers for furniture are out of style , the only solution is learn to remove that dastardly spot! Here is a general guide to removing stains from upholstered furniture:

1. Look on the furniture tag to determine the method of stain removal. Letters are used to tell you what cleaner will work best on your fabric:
   - W means spot clean with a water-based solution or mild detergent. It is best to use the foam produced by the solution to do the majority of the work.
   - S means spot clean with a solvent only in a well-ventilated room. Cleaning with solvents may cause spotting and any water stains may be permanent.
   - SW means spot clean with either solvent or water-based foam
   - X means you are out of luck! Vacuum only! Not a smart buy for families with children!
2. Remove excess soil or food product right away if possible! Kids are notorious about spilling things in between the sofa cushions where you find it months later! The longer a spill stays on the fabric, the harder it is to remove. Vacuum the fabric as soon as you can. If the spill is thick, scrape the excess spill with a dull spoon or table knife.
3. Find an inconspicuous spot to test your cleaner. The bottom hem of the back of the sofa is a good spot!
4. If the fabric can be cleaned with water, use one gallon cool or warm water to about 5 teaspoons of mild dishwashing liquid. If the spill is grease or something that has caramelized sugar, your solution should be 50% white vinegar and 50% water.

5. Don't over-wet the fabric. Let the foam of the solution do most of the work. Blot it frequently, whether you are using water or solvent, and work from the outer edge to the center of the spot to help prevent rings.
6. Don't rub the fabric too vigorously or it may pill.
7. Rinse the fabric with a clean sponge and clean water.
8. Blot the liquid with an absorbent material. Cotton towels or paper towels are great for this job. Some experts recommend placing a heavy weight over a thick layer of towels and replacing the towels periodically.

Remember vacuuming often is your first best defense against stains. Not only will it clean soil from your furniture, but it encourages you to check between those cushions and under those chair arms for food stains. Your second best defense is garbage bag slipcovers, but they may limit your decorating choices.

Few general rules for removing stains are given below:

1. Give your product time to work. Rubbing alcohol removes ink off most surfaces but not the minute you blot it on. Dab on your cleaner then allow a 30 minute wait. This gives the product time to dissolve the residue eliminating all the rubbing and scrubbing.
2. Always get to a spill immediately. The longer a spill sets the worse the stain.
3. Rinse the cleaner out of fabrics especially carpets with one-quarter cup white vinegar in two cups of water. Then repeat with plain water.
4. Blotting properly prevents fraying of fabric. Blot using a damp towel. Form a knuckle with your index finger and push into the towel. Rock you finger back and forth, move the towel then rock your finger left to right. Repeat. Reapply the cleaner if needed. After the

second application of cleaner, again make a knuckle with your index finger. Push your knuckle and the towel into the carpet then twist your wrist clockwise. Carpet fibers are twisted clockwise. This removes the stain from between the fibers without leaving them fuzzy.

5. Do not use heat of any kind even hot water. Heat sets stains. Dryer heat particularly means certain death for easy removal.
6. Put a clean rag under the fabric you are working on to prevent the stain from spreading to another surface.

Most stains land in 4 categories; food, grease etc., dirt and who knows. Throw in easy solutions for wax and gum and most perplexing problems tuck their tails and run.

Bleaching

Bleach causes the discoloration. Add one-half to 1 cup of hydrogen peroxide per regular washer. The first time allow the clothes to soak in the washer for 30 minutes. Then wash normally only use less detergent. White clothes return to their normal brightness and coloured cloths perk up as well. Add one quarter cup of baking soda to your washer for additional freshness.

Begin filling your washer with water. Add your detergent and peroxide then the clothes. The detergent can't clean unless it dissolves. Switch to liquid detergents for front loading washers. Fill your tub only three-quarters full. Clothes clean by the agitating action amongst themselves. Crowd them and this cleaning action comes to a halt. Pretreat most stains with a dab of liquid dish soap. Add a few squirts to a spray bottle filled with water. It's cheaper than prewash sprays, works better too.

Food stain. Food never spills down your front unless you are out in public where it quickly makes a mockery of your front side. Should, that happen, head to the closest restroom. Gently dab a bit of liquid soap on the spot and resist the temptation to rub. Let the soap set. It may look funny until you get home, but the food stain comes right out. Cherry popsicles are a favourite treat except when they land in your lap. Mix a 50/50 solution of hydrogen peroxide and cool water. Spray on and let it set 30 minutes. Rinse with a vinegar and water solution. It may take a treatment or two but it comes out. Peroxide is bleach, so always test a spot first. If a favourite shirt has an old stain, soak it in a 50/50 solution of peroxide and water for 30 minutes. It might surprise you and come out, even after going through the dryer.

Coffee, coke, mustard and the likes of whatever your dish soap doesn't remove: First dab on liquid dish soap and let that set several hours. Blot and rinse as above. If the stain insists on being stubborn, try foaming shaving cream. Spray on the spot, no need to rub it in, and wait 30 to 60 minutes. The gel shaving cream does not work so use foaming.

Grease and oil stain. Kitty litter will absorb most of the oil and grease. Apply and use a brush to work it into the concrete. In the evening, pour on concentrated orange cleaner letting it set overnight. It pulls any oil or grease to the surface. Use old towels to absorb what you can and hose down. Oil or grease on fabrics or other surfaces: Dab on a bit of a natural orange cleaner and let that set at least an hour. Then blot with a clean cloth. It may take a treatment or two, but it works. If you spill gasoline on your clothes or in your car, dispose of your clothing properly and replace the carpeting in your car. Gasoline and water don't mix making complete removal impossible. Gas spontaneously combusts especially when the weather turns hot. Always put a container of gas inside a plastic tub when carrying it in your car. If the tank spills over, the tub keeps the gas contained saving your carpet.

Ink. Rubbing alcohol does a great job every time. Remember to let the alcohol set for 30 minutes. If regular rubbing alcohol doesn't work ask your pharmacist for denatured alcohol.

Magic marker. Permanent magic markers mean just that. They are nearly impossible to remove. Try dabbing on a bit of concentrated orange cleaner. Let it set even overnight. Rinse to remove. Sometimes toothpaste will help lighten marker stains.

Dirt. Grass stains and knees. It's a given, walk across the lawn and they appear from nowhere. Immediately rub in some liquid dish soap, let it set overnight, wash as usual. Treat dirt or red clay on children's baseball uniforms in the same manner. For really stubborn spots mix a paste of dishwasher detergent and work in. Don't rub real hard, or you could damage the fabric.

Baseball caps. Wash on the top rack of your dishwasher. Remove before the dry cycle and air dry.

Gum and wax. Freeze gum with an ice cube. Ice hardens it making removal easy. Oh those dripless candles. They can and do drip, but nobody told you. First freeze the wax with an ice cube in a ziplock plastic bag. Then chip off as much as you can with the blunt side of a knife. Using a hair dryer and a plain white paper towel, heat the wax blotting with the paper towel as it melts. This works just fine for carpets as well as fabrics. Remember to put plastic under a fabric so the wax doesn't transfer to the other surface.

Underarm stains. Do not use this method on silk, wool or dry clean only fabrics. Always test a spot first for colour fastness. Hydrogen peroxide is bleach, it's safe but it is bleach and could discolour the fabric. Often using household bleach only causes stains to worsen. Hydrogen peroxide will not cause those problems. If you use a 3% peroxide found at grocery and drug stores it can be used full strength. Often a 50/50 solution of peroxide to water works just as well. If you use a 20 to 30% solution then dilute with water 1 part peroxide to 5 to 6 parts water. Pour the peroxide on the stain and allow to set 30 minutes. Then wash as normal using cool water. Air dry to make sure the stain has been completely removed. Heat sets a stain making it difficult to remove. If the stain is still present after 30 minutes use the peroxide full strength. If the shirt has odors as well as stains, then fill a sink with cool water adding 2 cups of peroxide and 1/2 cup of baking soda. Wait 30 minutes and launder.

Rust. Squeeze the juice from a lemon on the spot. Sprinkle on some salt and let it set several hours keeping the spot damp with lemon juice.

7

Interior Decoration

Interior decoration can be a big and expensive budget and it is always good to pre-plan and foresee the problems that may arise beforehand to prevent wastage of money, time and effort or a result that does not match to your original intentions or conflict with your daily needs. Choose the project that fits your budget. You may also want to beak up your total project plan in smaller and more manageable projects and then prioritize them to fit your budget. Mostly, people prefer to solve living problems first and targeting the areas that are most used or lived-in in the house. Décor themes and styles can be chosen from the interior décor magazines to make your hotel look bright, cheerful and casual or formal, elegant and sophisticates. You may also prefer rustic, country and shabby-chic styles.

Color schemes should be chosen according to your theme, climatic conditions, size of the room and light that comes in the room. Monochromatic walls can be made to look beautiful with accents in two or three accent colors. Prints of fabrics such as stripes, plaids, floral or checks can be used as single or mix-and-match according to your preference. For large rooms, choose multi-hued upholstery, bed linens and coverings, wallpaper and window curtains with a large-scale print. Contrasts of mid-scale and small-scale prints look too. Play with either color or print or texture. Variants of all can lead to chaotic feel. Solid colors or neutrals go well with patterns. Position your furniture into more than one group seating areas, if the room is big, use screens and area rugs to divide the areas and use warm colors all around to make it feel cozy.

Stick to less than three colors, prints or textures in a small room and keep your decorating muted for serenity. Mirrors reflect more light, and glass-to tables almost disappear from view making the space feel larger and airy. Tall vertical furniture, floor length curtains hung from ceiling height and vertical stripes add to the height of the ceiling. Use symmetrical décor elements such as a pair of lamps and vases for the formal look in a room. Smooth, glossy and plush are the key words to elegance, be it highly polished wooden furniture or luxurious carpeting. Casual decorating can use horizontal lines with low furniture line and use of different textures. Displaying your collectibles on wall mounted shelves and grouping pictures of different sizes on walls for an informal look, does well too. For collections, display heaviest piece at the bottom, groupings at the eye level and preferably in odd numbers.

Decorating Principles

Decorating any of the room depends on its color - pastel or bright and matte, egg-shell or glossy; focal point of the room such as a window with a great view, entertainment center, a beautiful vase or idol of Buddha; function(s) of the room - whether it is a bed room, drawing cum dining room study cum play room for kids; natural light coming in the room and its lighting system; and the traffic flow in the room, which is maximum in kitchen, bath and lobby. Here are some basic and important thumb rules and decorating principles to keep in mind before you start your hotel décor project:

— Use of the room decides the furniture that goes in it.

— A bedroom needs a bed, one or two nightstands, a dresser, chest of drawers closet and/or armoire and a chair or bench.

— Kids room may be a nursery with crib and changing table or for older children, needs to be equipped with a study desk, a shelf, rack or chest to keep their toys and playthings and may be bookshelves.

— Dining, breakfast or room where you eat must have a table and seats enough for all the daily users with options to expand to accommodate occasional guests. Extra chairs may be kept stacked in a corner when not in use.

— Family rooms, living rooms, entertainment room or place for casual gatherings should have comfortable seating arrangements, television, area for playing (depending on personal choice) and may be a computer to work or chat on. You may add fireplace for warmth and elegance.

— Potted or hanging plants and beautiful arranged flowers bring colors of Nature inside. Even a single rose in a sleek vase can spice up the table décor.

— Do not think that daily-use instruments such as taps, showers, cables, wires, switches and sockets do not need to be included in your color scheme. They can become powerful accents in the hands of a skilful detail-oriented interior designer and they are very much visible.

— Remember the color of the room affects your mood so choose them carefully according to your personality and if another room is visible through the room, try to create a harmony between their colors. Areas can be defined in a very large room with subtle changes in the color of walls.

— White walls can be a good backdrop for your artwork or display of collectibles.

— Light and cool colors seem to add space to the room while warm and dark colors shrink it and make them look cozy.

— Painting them in contrasting colors can highlight attractive architectural elements such as trims and moldings. However, it shrinks the space a little bit.

— Painting them in the same shades as the backgrounds can hide ugly elements. It opens up the space too.

— Color trends keep changing so opt for a classic palette appropriate for the size, comfort level and function of the room. You may experiment with furnishing and accessories.

— Direction in which the room is located in the hotel and that of the windows of the room determines the amount of sunlight that comes in the room and at what time. A window in the east brings in not-so-intense morning rays. You can use natural daylight to the utmost by assigning the rooms accordingly. A room to the east can be used for morning chores such as preparing and having tea and breakfast.

— Blinds are good choices as window treatments for rooms that get more natural daylight as they allow you to welcome it or shut it off, as you like.

— For evening gatherings, room with windows opening to the west is better as they allow you to have lovely sunset views. It can be used as family and living room or library. The light here plays along well with warm and rich colors.

— A room with windows to the south can work well as a green room and is good enough for indoor plants as it has more access to sun heat. Don't use accessories that will fade in sun here.

— Daylight does not flicker and is still provide more illumination than electricity, so make more use of it in daytime. It is diffused enough to not hurt the eyes. The constant pressure to adjust to the bright area of electric task lighting and shadows surrounding it can be harmful for these delicate organs.

— Artificial lighting is generally of two types - Incandescent lighting, which is warm and soft and Fluorescent lighting, which is harsh and glaring but focus-oriented.

— Make a focal point of the room with the help of rare pieces, beautiful collectibles or contrast in colors. Some sure shot focal points are fireplace, window views, tabletop fountain, burning candles, entertainment center, piano, bed, sword and shield, giant religious statue or anything that is out of the ordinary in the room.

— You may either highlight your primary and immovable focal point or distract the person with another focal point for a very large room.

— Keep the area with traffic flow free to avoid bumping into furniture. Furniture arrangement should allow people to move easily through the room, to the door, window and closet and make use of the furniture, dresser or drawer without any problem.

— Proper placement of furniture takes into account space available, size of furniture, the location of doorway, seating arrangement, obstructions, light fixtures and wiring.

— The thumb rule is that traffic flow should not have too many curves and bends. So work on it.

Tips For Decorating Hotels

Hotel décor needs to be well-planned including the budget available, priorities, floor plan, tools, equipments and supplies needed and actual purpose of the project including expansion of family, changing style and theme of hotel, repainting it or equipping it for specific cases such as kids, orderlies or disabled people along with making addition to the hotel and getting rid of moisture in hotels, so that you don't run into problems that you haven't thought of before. Here are some things that you need to keep in mind before you start working on the project:

— Write down the desired features and elements such as additional storage or change in furniture.

— Mark the options you can do yourself and you do not need to spend money on them such as rearranging the furniture and artwork and getting rid of clutter in one color.

— Use another color to mark the DIY options with small budget.

— The left-out items such as changing electrical and plumbing systems, major renovations and remodeling and installing high-tech intricate appliances may need professional help and more money, so you can prioritize them and implement them at your ease.

— Floor plans can be made by hand or using software. If the blueprint of the house is available, you can have exact structural, electrical and plumbing layouts and dimensions. Take into account measurements of walls, doors, windows, fireplace and other fixed.

— An interesting furniture arrangement idea with fireplace as focal point includes placement a pair of loveseats or a sofa, coffee table and two club chair set in front of the fire, facing each other.

— Sofa can be placed facing the fireplace, window or TV and then end tables and side tables can be kept according to the position of the sofa.

— There should be enough space to reach the dresser or closet in the bedroom, ideally two feet.

— For quality décor in small budget, it is best to do as much as you can on your own including buying the material you need.

— However, hire a professional for electrical and plumbing work for safety and quality work.

— Set aside some money for unexpected expenditure.

Hotel Decoration Ideas

Painting walls and hanging the wallpaper, are some of the wall decoration ideas for your hotel, that you can do yourself with a little help and advice from us. Here are some basics for you:

Painting

Remove everything from the room including furniture, floorings and switch covers or move them to the center center of the room. Then clean the walls, windows and trims with soap-water or diluted all-purpose cleaner thoroughly. Paint finishes range from flat to eggshell or matte to satin to semi-gloss, and gloss. All have their pros and cons. Flat paint is difficult to clean but good for hiding away dents in the wall. They are not preferred for kitchens, baths and high traffic areas. Eggshell finish is most suited to bedrooms, satin finish for fantasy décor while semi-gloss is easier to clean and thus, can be used for trims and walls of high traffic areas. Gloss finish is best to highlight trims and moldings and can be used for windows and doors too, for you can wipe finger marks on them by just swiping them with a rag. Good quality paints require less number of coats, are easier to apply and clean and last longer. For kids' room, you may choose an inexpensive variety for you may have to keep making changes to it according to the age and choices of a child. Use painter's tape to cover baseboards, window and door frames and molding edges before painting. Paint the ceiling first, followed by walls and then the trims and moldings. Holding a small container of paint in one hand makes painting faster.

Do not load the roller or brush with paint too much or it will drip. Use narrow brush for trims and angled brush to fill 'cut-in' edges. Be sure to clean your brushes after work outdoors. Water-soluble latex paint in the brush can be rinsed thoroughly in running water. Blot the water with paper towels and then keep them in a plastic wrap. You may need to use turpentine oil to clean oil or alkyd paints from the brush or roller. You nay also try your hand at faux painting and texture painting such as painting in stucco, suede, leather and other finishes but it needs much more expertise. Simple way to funk up your wall, window, door, cupboards and furniture painting is to use stencil painting.

Hanging Wallpaper

For wallpaper installation, you need to clean the walls thoroughly including crayon marks, scraping off loose paint and filling cracks and holes with spackling compound and smoothing them by rubbing them with a wallpaper when it is dry. Peel and remove the old wallpaper starting from seams and corners. If they are not removable, paint them with at least one coat of primer. Sand and scrape the adhesive and rinse the wall. Let it dry.

Calculate the dimensions of the wallpaper by measuring the distance from ceiling to floor and allow four inches extra for proper installation. There can be variations in the size of the walls on one room so measure them individually making note of the location of door or window in it. For perfect vertical alignment of wallpaper, it is better to draw lines with a pencil and then place the wallpaper edge along the line, pressing it with your palms or a roller press. Wallpaper with adhesives may need to be dampened with water before installation.

Other Options

Some other hotel décor ideas besides painting and wallpapering include giving a character to your fireplace by covering it with the desired stone finish, add wood panels and mouldings, large mirrors to makeup for the lack of windows and tiling the kitchen, baths, entryways and fireplaces. There are handmade tiles that can make your hotel look entirely different and conform it to a particular theme. Fabrics and upholstery invites elegance, soft and plush look and richness to the room while cork tiles will help you protect your secrets for sneaking neighbors as they are almost soundproof.

Hotel Decoration Tools

Every hotel decoration project makes use of many tools and having them ready at hand makes the work easier too. Tools to paint walls, install wallpaper, stripping furniture, wood molding and laying tiles have been discussed in this section.

Painting Tools

Good quality paint spreads more and results in long

lasting finishing and better results. Narrow brushes are better to paint trims and windows while one with an angled edge can help you cover 'cut in' around windows, doors and ceiling edges better. Wide and straight-edged brush is a wise choice for painting large walls and ceiling spaces and is easier to handle than rollers for beginners. The bristles of the brush can be natural or synthetic. Only oil-based or alkyd paints can use brushes with natural-bristles. Good quality brushes have flexible tips, split ends, tapered towards the center for smooth and even application of paint and the length of their bristles at least one and a half times of the width of the brush.

Good brushes apply paint in a thicker and smoother film than economy ones thus, give a uniform sheen, hides the faults and do not leave ridges or brush marks in the paint. Rollers usually have two parts - a plastic handle and its metal cover. Handles should be easily grip able and light enough to carry easily for long periods of time. Wider frames can be used for large spaces while smaller ones for trims and narrow spaces. To paint a ceiling, you may want a roller with the facility of a screwed-in extension. Synthetic covers are good for latex paint while natural ones can be used for oil-based paints.

Thin and smooth cover nap means smoother walls while textured walls such as stucco painting may need thicker and textured cover naps to hold more paint and get the desired effect. You may also need a step stool or a sturdy ladder while painting especially for ceiling edges and corners. Protect your eyes and hair with plastic cap and goggles and wear disposable gloves to protect your hands. Thin wood sticks to stir the paint, a roller tray with disposable liners, light bucket to carry paint, painter's tape, drop cloths to cover the floor and furniture of the room, spackling compound and a putty knife, sandpaper and rags to wipe your hands on are some other things while painting walls.

Tools for Wallpapering And Other Work

For hanging wallpaper, you need a large flat surface, ladder or stepstool, sponge or rags, scissors, pencil, measuring tape, drop cloths, craft knife with disposable blades, a level, a straightedge, a chalk line plumb and sandpaper along with wallpaper primer, adhesive, masking tape, plastic smoothing tool, water tray, seam roller and rolls of wallpaper. Cleaning the furniture and walls well make working on them much easier, whether it is painting, waxing or polishing them. To clean furniture, you will need toothbrush, soft club, toothpicks and steel wool for scrubbing and poking dirt from hidden corners. Be sure to use only those chemicals to clean that don't hurt your furniture, especially the wooden pieces. TSP pr tri sodium phosphate may soften a finish.

Wearing gloves and goggles and working in a room with proper ventilation will keep you safe too. For restoration and refinishing furniture, you may need paint stripper. Heavy bodied stripper is best for both vertical and horizontal surfaces while liquid stripper can be used to remove its residue. Dispose paint stripper residue carefully along with rags and towels used in the process as it is toxic and highly flammable in nature. Antique furniture should never be sanded but worked upon with good boiled linseed oil without the addition of polyurethane.

Hotel Accessories

It's not just about the beautiful palace that you crave for but also about the feelings attached to it that you value.

The colorful hotel accessories that were bought and the feelings and emotions that family members shared with each other is what makes the hotel more precious. The hotel witnesses a lot of happenings in our life a mixture of good and bad. Therefore while decorating the house, the focus should not just be on classy expensive hotel decoration pieces but on articles that add some personal touch to your hotel. Every household item should have some reflex ion of your personal taste.

While shopping for the colorful hotel accessories like lampshades, plants, fabrics, wallpapers and kitchenware etc, give due consideration to your personal choice. If you are designing your bedroom, then look out for things that go well with your personality. If you very jovial and bubbly kinds, then a lot of handcraft pieces would please you. Bright wall colors like red, blue or yellow with some artistic wooden lampshade will be apt. Fill the space with lot of colorful stuffed toys.

For an elderly person who is a nature lover, plants would be the best option to decorate. Nice cool fabrics and decent monochromatic color scheme would be perfect. If you are fond of accessorizing your room to such an extent that you don't feel the need to leave any corner untouched, then go in for decent wall colors like beige, fawn and crème that can accommodate all these decorative items. Whatever you choose, make sure it reflects your inner self.

Shoestring Budget and Hotel Décor

Creativity is not a slave of the wealthy and you can decorate hotels and make them look better and live more efficiently even without spending a fortune. However, this may need even more skill and hard labor so that you can do all the tangible things yourself to cut off the expenses of hiring a professional.

Here are some tips for hotel décor that can be done on a shoestring budget:

— For a particular look such as retro, minimalist and contemporary, colonial, American, country, art deco or funky 70s, search local flea markets and antique shows thoroughly or go for machine-made reproductions.

— Add molding to your ceiling for the traditional look. Layered moldings can simulate the look of richly carved crown moldings.

— Fake ceiling medallions, made of molded plastic compounds but look like plaster, are quiet cheap and interesting too.

— Try baseboard moldings to make your room ooze elegance and sophistication but keep away from plastic moldings here.

— Used panels to hide ugly walls or wainscot them 9paneling the bottom half of a wall) to add warmth to the room. You can also use bead boards for narrow slats placed evenly. Go cheaper with chair rails, painting the bottom half of the wall in a contemporary color and add a wallpaper border to it.

— Wall-to-wall carpeting can add color, warmth and texture to a dull and boring room and a thicker synthetic carpet can soundproof your apartment from nosy neighbors.

— Nylon floor carpets last longer and are easier to clean.

— Area rugs on a hardwood floor are less expensive and offer more decorating variety than wall-to-wall carpeting.

— Laminated floors can look like hardwood floor too.

— Floor tiles can make your floor look much more beautiful and you can also use it on countertops.

— Tiles come in different varieties such as clay based ones that are handmade, glazed, slippery, hard to clean but can last much longer; porcelain tiles that are hard and are colored well; terrazzo tiles made by setting marble or granite chips in concrete and polishing; terracotta tiles that are water and stain-resistant and are available in myriad of colors and styles. Choose ones that suit your purpose and budget.

— Sheet vinyl sheets and tiles can simulate almost anything and are thus very popular. They are easy to maintain too.

— Floating installation of laminate flooring are easily removable, scratch-resistant and easy to maintain but are not repairable and can get damaged by water.

— Cork tiles are inexpensive and warm but can be damaged by water too.

— Unlike sophisticated and expensive linoleum floors, concrete floors look earthy and rustic.

— Choose window treatments according to your privacy and light needs and you windows may be bare or have simple blinds and sheer curtains, if you have a great view outside.

— In bedrooms, you may want window treatments that block out light. Drapes and curtains with thermal linings keep rooms warmer in winter and cooler in summer.

— Mini-blinds are very cheap. Other types of blinds are wood blinds, faux wood blinds, metal, vinyl and fabric blinds and may be horizontal or vertical as you choose. There are shades too such as Roman shades that you can go through and coordinate with valances painted and sewn at hotel for the elegant look you desire.

Castle in a Loft

Live like a king or queen in a tiny loft by using easy ideas given here. These simple loft decorating and small apartment decorating ideas will actually seem to open up space and make life much more efficient:

— Most of the world's population lives in small to medium-sized hotels and efficient living that uses every inch of space usefully is a skill we need to master.

— Use space in such a way that you have more floor space and yet have all that comforts that make your hotel a place where you would like to live.

— Hotel should feel big and yet feel cozy enough.

— Dual-purpose, multi-purpose or versatile furniture pieces are a blessing in disguise to make your abode look stylish and be functional at the same time.

— Tall dressers, armoires and chest of drawers are an asset as they take less floor space and yet use the vertical space to provide you the needed storage area.

— Wall space becomes even more important in tiny hotels and shelves and racks attached to them are quite useful to display your collection, keep alarm clock and that sleek vase.

— Tables, ottomans, sofas and chairs with hidden storage areas can make your magazines and junk disappear and yet be available to you when you want to go through them.

— Folding chairs, tables and beds allow you to fold them and keep them leaning on to walls, out of your eyesight until you need them while entertaining guests or going to sleep in the night.

— You can use storage bins to keep some of the out-of-season things under the bed.

— Retractable doors take less space when they are open and thus, are an asset for corner décor or a very narrow lobby.

— If you have a very tiny room and you are not able to find the right size of study desk for it, you can try out kids' furniture store for the purpose.

— A movable sleek furniture on wheels can be used tactfully like having three small tables of same size and proportions that can be joined to form a longer table and detached to make use of them separately is much better when you have a very small room décor.

— A dining table with removable leaves and loveseats instead of sofas are better for loft living.

— Choose the focus of the room such as your entertainment area and place mirrors to reflect it. Mirrors are useful accents for small spaces that add light and depth to the room.

Choosing Beds

Standard sized beds are generally categorized as single, twin, extra-long twin, full, double, queen, king, California king, eastern king and western king that have their own distinctive and defined bed sizes. One can choose from amongst them according to their need, number of people they need to accommodate in a room, size of the persons and size of the room itself. Just a little difference in size can get you cheated by lots of bucks, so read this guide to more about these bed types, before choosing one for your bedroom, children's room or guest room:

— Custom-sized beds may look good in a room but then you will always need custom-sized bedding for the perfect fit.

— Twin beds are nothing but single beds that are narrower and can fit into tiniest bedrooms. They are good choices for kids' room or guest room and often come as bunk beds or have 'trundle' fitted under them that can be pulled out to accommodate a sleepover friends. They are 39" wide and about 75" long. Their bedsheets are easily available but it may be too short for some adults.

— Extra long twin beds are 39" wide like a twin bed but is 80" in length to accommodate tall teenagers and adults and are favorite choices for college dorm rooms or attic rooms for singles. However, finding bedding for it can be bit of a headache.

— It is not necessary that 'standard' beds and bedding sizes is same everywhere so it is advisable to have the exact measurements with you for better fittings.

— Double or full sized beds are one and the same thing and are 54" wide and 75" long, which gives only 27" of space per person, which is 12" less than a twin bed and thus are considered too narrow for daily purposes. However, they still require small space and thus may be used in smaller rooms or for guest rooms.

— Double and full sized beds may be too short for some adults.

— Queen beds are 60" wide and 80" long and thus, allow each person 30" of space, which is still much less than the one offered by the twin bed. However, couples often prefer to use it because it occupies less floor area and fit snugly into small master bedrooms of new couples or guest rooms.

— An 'Olympic queen' bed is slightly bigger than the standard queen size but then neither queen-sized not king-sized bedding will not fit it correctly.

— Standard King bed or Eastern King bed is 76" wide and 80" long and allows for 38" of space per person for a couple, while California or Western King bed is

72" wide and 84" long, allowing 36" of width per person and more vertical space for taller persons.

— You can also opt for two extra-long twin beds instead on one standard sized king bed to allow greater versatility.

— You may need to search for right fit of sheets before buying one.

— Most of the king-sized beds come with half-width box springs and one mattress to allow for easier moving and changing position.

Decorating Balcony

The smallest balcony can be turned into a cozy retreat with imagination, few potted plants and chairs. Hide the junk behind a bench, lattice screen or shrubs and choose plants and accessories that can thrive well for long time and do not need constant care. Shade plants for balconies where sunrays hardly reach and accessories that do not crack or fade in the sunny balconies are not so hard to find after all. Here are some other tips that you can use for decorating balcony, patio and deck in your small apartment:

— Divide a large and wide balcony into smaller areas to add more rooms to your hotel that you can use as dining area, private library or a small garden.

— Experiment with bold colors here and make it a family seating area where everybody can have coffee and gossip for a few minutes every evening.

— You can also use balcony or patio as an ever-ready venue for your fun barbecue parties, turn it into an exotic garden with big bright flowering plants or install a small pond or fountain there surrounded by small bonsai plants.

— Balconies can become a great place to meditate and worship in private. You may need to cover it with bamboo screens however. Try this one out.

— A screen of ivy complete with birdhouses and birdbaths will lend the look of English garden to your balcony.

— Furniture for balcony can range from a porch swing to two or three chairs with a coffee table or just a chaise lounge or a bench with a side table.

Handling Space Issues

It is not always an asset to have a large house to live life peacefully and serenely. In fact, a room larger than you actually need becomes a burden and needs much more maintenance, cleaning, dusting, mopping, washing, ironing and polishing. We have some good advice that deals with space issues and how to handle rooms with different shapes and areas while decorating. It gives you and idea on how to rearrange your room to make better use of space and shape of the room:

— Evaluate the shape of your room as square, rectangular or L-shape; your personality traits as Victorian, French, rustic, modernistic, high-tech, Oriental or Zen-like; room problems in terms of being narrow, having low ceiling, architecturally sterile or too long and room assets as having a focal point in terms of mirror or a fireplace, a window with beautiful views or delicate moldings before you start decorating it.

— Make a room plan beforehand including doors, windows and things attached permanently to the wall. You can use a scale of ¼″ to 1'.

— Make cutouts of the furniture you want to put in the room using the same scale as of the room floor plan and try to visualize the room by placing them in the plan. 3-D virtual plans on computer can give you better idea about the personality and look of the room.

— Keep the pathways to move between the furniture pieces free.

— Match the type of furniture to the architectural elements of the room keeping in mind the focal point of the room.

— A bland room can be funked up with paneling, stenciling, using chair rails, shoji screens or even French doors.

— A room with low ceiling needs low furniture lines, tall dressers or armoires that go all the way to the ceiling and vertical stripes on wallpaper. You may also create the illusion of taller room by painting same shade of light and cool color on walls and ceiling delineation.

— For very narrow and long rooms, use warm dark and matte colors on shorter walls and light and cool colors on longer walls.

— Use versatile furniture with hidden storage space.

— Rooms with odd shapes and off-center focal point can be divided into smaller areas that can be managed better and allot a focal point for each. Area rugs, screens and dividers, subtle hints such as change in scale of patterns on wallpaper or slight difference in color of walls can be used to give more definition to these separate areas.

Seasonal Decoration

Every season has a flavor and we Indians are fortunate enough to enjoy four seasons namely spring, summer, autumn, and winter. Seasonal decoration adds charm to your hotel by giving it a new fresh look. This is the time to show your creativity and come up with innovative ideas. It's all about experimenting with different colors, fabrics, furnishings etc and your room gets a season perfect look. Light colors for summers and warm bright colors for winters look fabulous.

For summer decorating, you can check out some cool motifs in bed sheets. Floral prints can be a great choice. Look out for lighter shades like baby pink, sea green and ocean blue. Neutral shades can also be tried. Experiment with bed sheets, pillow covers etc. give the greenhouse effect to your house by placing money plants at different spots and try out a cool light shade. Monochromatic color scheme with everything matching matching can add that dazzling effect. Try fixing up to a single theme of background color. Silk and cotton fabric is just apt for that soft, mushy feel. Clear crystal vases look fantastic at the corners of your living room.

For winter home décor, the best deal is to play with some nice bright colors in heavy fabric that bring warmth and coziness. Wooden articles at the corners, beautiful lampshades and lots of cushions will embellish the beauty of your living room. Brass items and the pottery containers will look simply awesome. For dining room, try out some antique flower vases. Jute tablemats can give a refreshing look. Replace your floral print crockery with holiday designs. Leave the monochromatic color scheme in winters and try out the multicolored theme with lots of bright rainbow colors. Give your hotel a new look this season giving a practical shape to your creativity.

A couple of days before the Christmas season sets in, people begin to come up with distinctive decorative ideas. While starting off with Christmas decoration, it is wise to set up your budget and decide on the theme on which you would be working. Budget seasonal décor is well planned and leads to more concrete decorative ideas. Here are a couple of tips for decorating your hotel:

— Set a theme and embellish in accordance with it. You can follow either a monochromatic theme or multicolored scheme. Flowers can be a good theme.

— Small artistic items add to the beauty of the house. Like Christmas is more associated with X Mas tree, stockings, Santa Claus, small gifts, stars, beautiful candles etc. Try these small decorative items using your creativity. There is a wide range of glaze papers, sketch pens and glittery sparkles.

— Beautify the Christmas tree. Cut the cardboard in different shapes and sizes and prepare gift boxes and stars and flowers and attach it on the branches of the X Mas tree.

— Colorful stockings are very easy to prepare. People who are good at stitching and knitting, this is the apt time to show your talent.

— Teddy bears and dolls are the best option if you have chosen a Toyland theme. Dress these teddies in pretty clothes. Tie colored ribbons around their neck. Give a nice hairstyle to your Barbie doll. Stuffed toys are the best way of decorating kids room.

— These days' artistic candles are selling like hot cakes. You can easily prepare them at hotel.

— Christmas preparation is incomplete without a cake. Do the topping with gems, nutties, dry fruits etc.

Decorating for Summer

Budget seasonal renovation can be very exciting and relaxing. Summer decoration helps you create a cool summer hotel and at the same time lends you a golden opportunity to show your creativity. Give an eye soothing effect to your hotel this summer. It's an interplay of colors and fabrics that can change the very look of your house.

Avoid patchy look as it brings warmth. Maintain fewer items in your room, as it will make your room look bigger. Wooden lampshades are a no for summers. To beat the summer heat, give a natural appearance by using varied types of plants and flowers. Flowers can be a good theme in summers.

Try out different light colors like baby pink, sky blue etc. If you want bright shades then opt for their pastel shades or else go in for neutrals. Brass items should be replaced with clear crystals. Give different cool flooring styles. Wooden or Bamboo flooring needs to be changed. The best way is to go in for bare floors.

Wall paint is the most prominent when someone enters the room. So, give your wall a refreshing feel. You can try out some light wall colors like beige, fawn and light pink etc. If you've got your walls painted in the last season only, then you can try out different simple designs in wallpapers. Don't hang too many things on the wall. You can use one or two walls for hanging beautiful sceneries, calendar etc.

Keep the windows open for the cool airy effect and remove all dark bright colored stuff. Check out some light cool fabric bed sheets and pillow covers. Place the furniture against the wall. It gives a bigger and a cozier look. So, this season give your house a makeover and see it will also enlighten your mood and bring magic to your life.

Every season has its own mood and flavor. Renovation is not all about the expensive items but about different creative decoration ideas that can give a new refreshing look to your house. You might have the best of furnishings but if they are not in harmony, it will spoil the whole look. Summers demand a cool and cozy look while winters demand bright war appearance. Seasonal decorating can be fun and challenging at the same time.

Certain tips on hotel décor need to be kept in mind while beautifying your house. Kids room can be given a makeover with the use of lot of bright colors. Colorful bedsheets with lacy pillows are just apt. A couple of festival cards can be glued on to the wall. Stuff toys like cute chubby teddy bears with long ears and pretty Barbie dolls can be placed at different corners. Parent's bedroom can be decorated with artistic jute bags and watercolor paintings. Wooden lampshades can be used to embellish the corners.

Dining room and living room can be given a new look by placing high craftsmanship flowervases. In autumn season, artificial flowers available in different colors and types can be used. Fragrance of fresh flowers can be used to your advantage. These days, the latest trend is of money plants in the drawing room. Colored chandeliers look fabulous and innovative. Showcase can be prettified with artistic antique wooden pieces. In dining room, you can use different tablemats. For bathrooms, look out for some cool colored hand towels. In winters experiment some warm bright colors. Now give your sweet hotel a new makeover.

Natural Hotel Décor

Autumn hotel decoration can be a great fun. Well, when it comes to autumn seasonal décor, natural styling is the best bet. Natural hotel décor adds liveliness to your house and gives a feel of the fall season. It's a time when everybody prepares themselves for the arrival of cold winters. Nature is full of beautiful things and this is the season when you can use glimpses of nature to your advantage. This is an absolutely inexpensive decorating, which requires you to use the different natural elements creatively.

You will be astonished to see how these deadwood, dried flowers and other fallen things can embellish your hotel. The list of such items is extensive and encompasses many unique varied things like pinecones, sticks, shells, cocoons, acorns, bird nests etc. All you need to do is to open your eyes and capture this natural beauty. Beautiful flowers can be tried out to adorn the rooms. You can prepare a bouquet of different bright flowers like sunflower, cosmos, zinnias and our all time favorite roses.

Dried grass can be placed in flower vases and used decoratively. Prettify gas jars with leaves and dry flowers. Candles can be made more decorative. Tie ribbons on the top or else at the middle. You can paint the candle. Candle can be used as a centerpiece on the dining table and around it place bowls again beautified with grains and leaves. Use your old clothing, waste stuff, newspapers etc to wrap the wooden bowls. So, try out different creative ideas and give your house a new fresh seasonal look.

Winter Decoration

Give a warm and cozy look to your house this winter using you creative ideas. Warm winter décor will add on special effects and give your cozy winter house more warmth. Here are a couple of tips on winter hotel decoration:

— Use heavy fabrics to add on more warmth. Velvet is apt for the soft mushy feel. Look out for bed sheets and cushions in vibrant rainbow colors. Add on multiple cushions as they add on to the cozy feeling.

— Bonfire can be created somewhere in the corner. Fire color looks simply mind-blowing and also helps boosting up the mood for romance.

— Wooden lampshades and bright antique pieces in the drawing room will do wonders.

— Handmade paintings and other intricate craftsmanship can be used to your advantage.

— If you are fond of pottery, then this is the time to showoff your skills and embellish the beauty of your rooms.

— Try out a bright wall paint like sunflower yellow, ruby pink etc.

— Ensure closeness in terms of furnishings for a cozier feel.

— Kids room can be decorated with lots of stuff toys. Toy theme would work well for kids room. Hang on more of colorful posters and paintings.

— Jute, a packing material can be used efficiently in making jute bags and jute mats.

— Embroideries of various kinds can sail smoothly in winters and find place on all types of beddings.

— Bamboo floorings can be a good choice.

— Furs and velvets are just too apt for the season.

— Check out heavy blankets and quilts in bright colors that are soft in touch but warm in feel.

— Lot of innovation can be done with photo frames. Change the pictures every season and place something that can go well with the room theme and one, which is consistent with season.

Give your hotel a makeover this winter and see its amazing effects.

Hotel Storage Solutions

Use various hotel accessories easily available in the market to organize things in your hotel and you will be able to display all the items that you collected over the years. You will be able to arrange things you need in a manner that is easily accessible. Here are few items you can use in your hotel:

— Use a metal towel rack either next to your shower or behind your bathroom door to store washcloths and small towels.

— Use a set of pockets made of plastic inside your kitchen cabinet door to store your spices.

— Instead of using filing cabinets hang acrylic wall pockets in your office to save space.

— Store seasonal clothing in bins under the bed, where it easily accessible when the weather changes.

— Hang simple mesh laundry bags behind your bathroom door and bedroom door to store dirty clothes.

— Use the inside of the broom closet to store gifts that you buy round the year to gift to family and friends as and when required.

— Use metal storage racks to keep things that you need to get easily for example in the bathroom a small metal rack can hold your toothbrush, toothpaste, face wash etc.

— Use canvas shoe bags inside you cupboard door to store things. This convenient and neat method to store things that you need regularly. For example use a shoe bag in the bathroom can hold shampoo, conditioners and other toiletries. Use one the children's cupboard to keep their toys, dolls etc. Use one in the cleaning closet to keep cleaning detergents. You could select a shoe bag that has see-through pouches.

Make optimal use of the storage space you have at hotel to keep things in an orderly fashion and to display things you love. Use metal racks, pockets, hooks and you will find that, you have all the place you needed, to you keep your things in a neat and accessible manner.

Organized Storage

Everybody likes things to be stored in an organized and neat manner so that, they can get what they want immediately, without having to look for it in all the cupboards at hotel. Cleaning, organizing and storing things is a tedious, difficult and uninteresting. But this job too needs to be done, so when you get down to doing it remember these tips:

— Carefully assess all the places in the house that can be used to store things.

— Before you actually begin, plan what you will store in each shelf, cupboard and closet. Each of these must be used to store specific things. After storing label them so that everyone knows the new location and gets used to it.

— Things that family members need frequently and use regularly should be easily accessible. Things that are not used regularly should be kept in places that not easily reachable.

— Organize all similar things together. For example winter clothes in a closet together, everyday china together, outdoor shoes together etc.

— Thoroughly clean your house twice a year, to get rid of things you do not want and to reorganize.

— Place things that are unattractive in closed closets or hide them behind something more attractive or put them in a bag and store.
— If you are using boxes to store things then label them and mention what is inside them.
— Allow enough space for future storage needs.
— Note down rooms with storage shortage and write down suggestions on how to increase storage.
— Make sure that you arrange everything in a neat and orderly fashion and keep all items required for one activity together. Example all sports related things in one closet using different shelves.

Types of Storage

When you are planning to clean and reorganize your house from top to bottom, it is important to have a clean idea about the different ways of storing things at hotel. By cleverly combining different methods of storing you can optimally use the space that you have. Here are a few storage methods:

— *Storing things in open units.* This method makes use of open storage shelves, glass cabinets and tabletops. Things should be arranged in an extremely neat and clean fashion, as everything will be visible. Unsightly things should be put into boxes and these should be neatly arranged on the shelves. The important thing is that all items stored in this manner must be organized and presentable.
— *Storing things in closed units.* Uses chest, cupboards, drawers under beds etc. Things that get untidy easily like clothes, office supplies; food supplies etc. are stored in this manner so that they are not visible to all and sundry. Things that are not used frequently

or are used seasonally are also stored in this way, in order to store them carefully till they are used again.

— *Storing things conveniently.* Things that are frequently and regularly used, should be stored in such a way that, they are easily accessible to everyone as and when needed. Things should be stored in their respective places, things required in the bedroom should be kept there and things required for cooking should be in the kitchen storage shelves. Things that you use often should be kept in top drawers of storage shelves and things not used often should be kept in the lower drawers. Keeping frequently used things in a convenient place in the house is important.

— *Storing things in remote spaces.* Items that are rarely used, seasonally used, those that are of no use at the moment but maybe of use later on etc. should be stored in places that are least accessible like the attic storage shelves, basement storage shelves and storage cupboards in the garage etc. Things like files or books that need to be referred to later on, Christmas decorations, artwork that the children have made over the years etc. can be stored in these remote areas.

Chest of Drawers

There is one piece of furniture in the house that can used to store things inside and display things of on top- it is a chest of drawers. A chest of drawers occupies very little place, can be used in any part of the house and can be used to store anything from clothes to photo albums to office supplies. At the same time the top can be used to display photos, plants or used as a TV table or to keep cosmetics that you use everyday. The chest comes in different types craved ones for the vintage look, country pine chests for the simple, clean look and the contemporary ones that are painted. When you are buying a chest look for a style and size that can be put to different uses over the years to come. The chest of drawers can be put to a number of uses. Here are a few tips on different ways to use the same chest:

— In the bedroom use the chest to keep clothes that you use at hotel, hosiery, under garments etc.

— Place it at entrance of the house to store hats, carves, gloves, mail, mufflers etc. You could place a mirror over the chest and place a vase with fresh flowers on the chest making it a lovely entry table.

— Use to store all things required for stitching and mending clothes. Threads, needles, lace, scissors, clothes that need mending can be kept in a separate drawer and those that need ironing can be kept separately as well.

— Use the chest as a side table in the dinning room, store napkins, cutlery, table mats, table covers etc. Arrange your china on top or place a flower arrangement on top of the chest.

— Use it to store things that you will need to pick up as you leave the house. Mittens, mufflers, hats etc. Place a soft board on top of the chest which can be used to pin up messages, reminder notes, bills that need paying etc. You could hang a row of hooks for your coats and jackets next to it.

— Use it in the drawing room to store coasters, the remote contorts, CDs etc. and display photographs, art pieces, plants or place the telephone on it.

— While the chest can be used to store clothes in the bedroom or guestroom the top can be used as a TV table. Some place in the chest can hold the remote controls, TV guides etc.

— Use the chest in the bedroom as a night table. On top of the chest place a lamp, along with books, magazines and bedtime reading material. Use top drawer to keep torch, some medicines, tissues etc. The rest of the chest can be used for clothes.

— Use one of the chests at hotel to store things required for wrapping gifts. Colored paper, ribbons, scotch tape, scissors, empty cards etc.

— Use the chest to store your baby's clothes, nappies, mats, washcloths, toys etc. On the top spread a mat made of soft cotton and use it to lay your baby on while changing his nappies.

— Use a chest to store all your photographs, photo albums, etc. Store pictures in them till you find time to arrange them in an album.

— Use a chest in a large bathroom to add character and store towels, bathrobes, toiletries, baby's bath toys etc. Place a potted plant on the top.

Hotel Lighting

Lighting is an important part of hotel décor and your room can look entirely different with changing lighting systems. In this section we will cover some major topics related to lights and lighting trends that are in vogue these days and help you to decide on the best-available options that satisfy your needs and desires. You will know how to hang a ceiling medallion and a chandelier and more about ceiling fan lighting to add elegance and sophistication to your room. Decorative lighting in rooms, how to choose decorative lights and lamps for different rooms and playing up an interesting accent in the room by down-lighting or up-lighting can make simplest of rooms look much more inviting and dramatic.

Dimmers and mood lighting is the latest trend in fashion. Here are tips to save electricity for you to read, a very contemporary topic indeed. Know what kinds of lighting trends are prevalent for kitchens these days. Landscape lighting can make your views look entirely different and give you an idea on how to incorporate Nature in your lighting style. Lights for outdoors should be enough to allow you to see what's around you and may be arranged according to the use of your outdoors. Backyards with a tennis court have different lighting requirements than a small garden with a coffee table and seating arrangement for family. Similarly, Feng Shui has its own rules regarding lighting that has some pretty practical tips included. So, go through that article once too.

Ceiling Medallion

Ceiling medallions are easy to fix light equipment, which can be painted to match, the color scheme of the room in which they are installed. These can be easily fixed to the ceiling with glue or drywall screws. Since these are relatively inexpensive and durable they can be used all round the house. Given below are tips on how to fix a ceiling medallion:

— While fixing a new medallion, the first thing you should do is to turn off the power from the fuse box.

— Arrange the medallion pieces on the floor and understand how the different pieces are to be fixed.

— If the ceiling opening is large you may have to increase the size of the medallion opening.

— Apply just enough glue, on to the back of the medallion, about one inch from the edge of the medallion.

— Set the medallion in its place and allow the glue about two hours to dry completely.

— Apply caulk around the medallion to cover any gap between it and the ceiling.

— Once a caulk has dried you can paint the medallion to match the color of the walls or ceiling.

— You can then wire and hang the chandelier or other ceiling light fixture, by attaching the ceiling cap to the surface of the medallion.

— If a ceiling light already exists and you want to install a medallion, you will have to remove the light fixture first and install the medallion. Once the medallion has been fixed properly, the light can be reinstalled.

— If you are reinstalling light fixtures ensure that you keep all the nuts and screws carefully, to reuse later on.

— You can clean your light fixtures thoroughly as you are dismantling them.

Hanging Chandelier

One of the most beautiful, elegant and dainty form of lighting is chandelier lighting. A chandelier of the right kind and size can add a whole new dimension to a room. There is no doubt that a chandelier light adds to the elegance of a room. For the chandelier lighting to have the right impact on the room and its décor, the chandelier light must be hung properly. Here are a few tips to follow while hanging a chandelier light:

— A chandelier being hung in the dinning room must be placed in the middle of the dinning table and the room.

— It is best to buy a chandelier that is about a foot smaller that your dinning table.

— It must be placed at a distance of at about 48 inches from the edges of the room.

— If your ceiling is 8 feet high then the chandelier should be hung about 30 to34 inches above the dinning table.

— Light from the chandelier bulbs that are just above a person can be hot and uncomfortable.

— Do not use bulbs with high wattage, as they will cause excessive heat.

— Use a wall dimmer to control the intensity of light and to set the mood.

— Placing a chandelier in a lobby or foyer is an excellent way of demarking the interior of the house from the exterior.

— While fixing a chandelier in the foyer hang it at a height that it illuminates stairways clearly.

— Chandeliers hung in the lobby can be broad and longer than ones used in dinning rooms.

— Conceal the wire or chain of the chandelier with some pretty fabric. Use fabric that is thrice as long as the chain and it will give the chain a beautiful bunched up appearance.

— If you are finding it difficult to hang the chandelier ask your electrician to install it.

Decorative Lighting

Using decorative lighting is another way of enhancing the beauty and character of the house. Earlier on lighting was done from the functional point of view. Today hotelowners want their lighting fixtures both interior and exterior to make a statement. More so the interior lighting. They select interior lighting fixtures to match the rest of the décor. Decorating hotels with elegant and tasteful light fixtures is a must these days. Decorative hotel lighting fixtures come in different shapes, sizes, finishes and materials. There are a wide variety of finishes to choose from. Some of the most popular ones are:

— Lamps that have a brushed nickel, stainless steel and copper finish, have become popular displacing the old favorite that was brass finished. These new finishes easily blend with the multi-colored décor of modern houses.

— Some lamps are finished in different colors and the consumer can choose one that exactly matches his needs. These are painted and may be textured or have silver and gold flecks.

— Another much in demand finish to the one that gives an antique and timeless look. This finish gives the lamps a very conventional look.

— Today a lot of attention is paid to detailing. Every aspect of the lamp is made decorative that gives the fixture more style and elegance.

The market flooded with a variety of decorative lighting fixtures. Selecting ones that are both functional and decorative can be a difficult task. Here are a few tips that to follow while choosing decorative lights:

— Employ a certified lighting consultant. He will help you find lamps that are functional and decorative.

— It you have a picture, of what the lighting fixture should look like, take it with you while shopping for fixtures.

— Plan a budget and decide by how much, you are willing to exceed that budget, for something you really want.

— While buying lighting fixtures for rooms bring something that matches the color of the walls. This will make it easier to find lights that match the rest of the décor.

— If you are looking for something specific and cannot find it, then you can get it specially made to order.

— While buying decorative lighting fixtures do not forget the practical purpose of lighting the room.

Dimmers For Lights

Today lights are not just used to brighten a dark room and help you see clearly in the dark. By adjusting lights we can meet the lighting specifications and requirements of the different people in the house. Lights can be adjusted according to the lighting needs of the task being performed. Lights can be adjusted by using dimmers. Dimmers increase the life of incandescent lamps as well. By making small alterations in the lighting system, you can manipulate the lights, to set the mood in the room. This can highlight the décor of the room as well. Dimmers are easy to install and can be fixed into the existing system or into a new system. There are different types of dimmers are available in the market:

- While using integrated dimming systems, the owner can make a series of pre decided lighting settings for each room. As and when required, the owner can evoke any of the pre-decided settings, at the touch of a button on the wall box or on a remote control.
- Touch dimmers change lighting at the touch of a button. At the touch of a button the owner can return to the previous light setting. Dimmers may even have a lighted indicator to show the strength of the present setting.
- Slide dimmers use manual control to set the lighting in a room. In these too at the touch of a button the owner can return to the earlier light setting.
- Rotary dimmers have manual dials that can be altered by turning the dial, to change the light setting. Some have a button control, which allows the owner to turn off the lights while, retaining the present setting.

Fluorescent lights can be dimmed, but they will not have the same effect as incandescent bulbs. It is cheaper and more suitable to use dim fluorescent lighting around the house. To alter fluorescent lighting you need specific fixtures and compatible dimming systems. Altering fluorescent lighting is more expensive that controlling normal lighting. It is most economical to install a custom system to control lighting throughout the house. It is possible to insert a house lighting system into an existing house. The cost of a lighting control system depends on how technologically advanced it is.

The way a dimmer works is fairly simple. A dimmer controls the amount of electricity that reaches the light. Lower the amount of electricity used lower the electricity bill. Dimming lights also increases the life of incandescent bulbs but not of fluorescent bulbs. Illumination can dictate the kind of activity that takes place in a room. Brightly lit rooms are for activity and dimly lit rooms are for relaxing. Using the right kind of lighting can enhance a room's décor. Using dimmers will no doubt reduce your electricity bill. Here are a few more tips to save electricity:

— Turn off lights when not in use.

— For outdoor lighting try using timers so that they turn on and off automatically. You could use photoelectric cells for lighting.

— Use reflectors bulbs for work related lighting.

— Use fluorescent bulbs wherever possible as, they use less electricity than incandescent bulbs, to produce the same amount of light.

Ceiling Fan Lighting

Gone are the days when ceiling fans were plain white in color and were only used to cool a room. Today fans come in trendy designs, to match different kinds of décor used in houses. Ceiling fans with lights are used for fancy lighting these days. The light on the ceiling fan attracts the maximum attention when anyone walks into a room. Lighting ceiling fans are often bought to replace light fixtures. They come in a numerous designs, which can be used to, match the décor of the room. Some of them are intricately carved blades, some finished in a way to give it an antique look and others that are very Victorian in style. Lighting ceiling fans come in bold and bright colors too. You can choose a color that matches the room.

Some fans come with lamps while in some you can choose the lamps. While selecting lights for your fan, ensure that the light is appropriate for that room. You require bright lighting in work areas like the kitchen and study and dim lighting will do in the bedrooms and dinning area. By installing a dimmer you can adjust the intensity of the light on the fan to suit your mood. Some fans come with remotes, not only to operate the fan but to operate the lights as well. A lamp lighting ceiling fan that is tastefully designed can be a decorative addition to the room. While buying ceiling fans remember to buy the best quality you can afford.

Kitchen Lighting

The kitchen is no longer a room in which you cook meals. The kitchen has become more and more of a family room, where the family gathers at least twice a day. The family members read the morning newspaper in the kitchen, meals for just the family are served in the kitchen, the children do their hotelwork on the kitchen table and bills are sorted out and checks written out there. If the kitchen is big enough it can be used to entertain guests as well. Therefore the kitchen must be adequately lit to enable these activities to take place without any hindrance. The kitchen is no longer lit with a single ceiling light fixture. Today the market is flooded with a variety of kitchen lighting fixtures. Here are a few tips to remember while lighting the kitchen:

— The size of the kitchen must be taken into consideration while deciding the lighting options.

— Ensure that the main work areas in the kitchen are well lit. The stove and sink areas must be well lit to enable you to work comfortably. You can use task lighting for these areas.

— The kitchen table is one of the focal points in the kitchen. Most of the activities other than cooking takes place here. Use a pendant or chandelier fixture to brightly lit up the table. Install a dimmer to the controls of this light and it can be used to change to mood while dinning. This fixture can add style to the kitchen as well.

— Install lights above and below the cabinets. The lights below the cabinet will highlight countertop of the kitchen. The lights above the kitchen will not only illuminate your attractive cabinets but will remove shadows from the kitchen.

— If you have a computer or a TV in you kitchen, you will have to provide special lighting in an effective manner, so that there is no glare on the screen.

— It is best to use dimmers for all the lights as they not only save electricity, but also allow you to set the mood in the kitchen.

— Using colored lights for the kitchen is very popular. Use lights of the same color for all the kitchen lighting.

— You can use decorative lights, which come in a number of finishes like wrought iron, rust, nickel etc.

— It is best if you can engage the services of a specialist or professional in this area.

You should be able to decide the kind of lighting you want for your kitchen after reading these kitchen lighting ideas.

Lighting Feng Shui Style

Feng shui is an ancient Chinese practice, which teaches an individual to live in harmony with one's surroundings, in order to increase the flow of positive energy and to have a positive state of mind. In the West leading a life based on the principles of Feng shui has increased in the recent times. The followers of feng shui use a number of procedures to get an idea of the energy of the surroundings and then alter it to suit the people living there. This ideology can be used to ensure that energy or "chi" flows freely in the surroundings thus making the people in that place happier and more positive in their outlook. The principles of feng shui can be applied to lighting as well. Here are a few tips to follow to light your house based on these principles:

— Shadows must not be cast while we read or cook food. So ensure that your study and kitchen is well lit with incandescent bulbs or halogen lights.

— Different colored lights denote different moods. Pinks have a calming effect; purple is used for passion, yellow for a relaxed feeling.

— Soft lights create positive energy, therefore when you need a lot of light for a particular room, use two soft light.

— Paper and cloth lampshades make the light appear softer and create a quiet atmosphere. Metal shades or shades that reflect light create an active atmosphere.

Use these shades in different rooms according to the mood you want to create.

— Using red lampshades in the living room brings fame.

— Use pink shades in the bedroom to increase romance in your life.

— Using purple shades in the office will increase wealth.

— Soften sharp corners of a room using accent lighting. Softening of sharp edges increases the energy flow and crates a relaxed atmosphere.

— Use uplighting to light up dark corners and beams so that the effect of negative energy is reduced.

— Well-lit areas encourage the flow of positive energy. Place mirrors in dark rooms or corners so that they will reflect light and positive energy will flow freely.

— Place a red colored crystal chandelier in the beginning or at the end of the room. This will increase the flow of energy.

— In rooms with irregular shapes place a lamp in the area that is missing to allow positive flow of energy.

— Channelize useful energy from the earth in the garden by using a pole light with the lamp on top. This will bring good fortune as well.

— Place a metal lamp with a white shade, in the western corner of a room, to increase your creativity.

— Using dimmers will not only create the right mood but positive energy as well.

Follow these simple tips to change the lighting of your rooms and there will be an increase in the amount of happiness and harmony in your house.

Landscape Lighting

Earlier the garden or outdoors was lit up, to allow people

entering the house after dark to see clearly and to prevent thefts. Today landscape lighting is done to enhance the beauty of the garden. Landscape lighting has become a work of art. The aim of landscape lighting is to display the house and the garden in its entire splendor after dark. The lighting has its functional aspect as well as it provides well lit outdoors which help prevent thefts. Here are a few tips for better landscape lighting:

— Use a professional, a certified lighting consultant who will be able to give you the best advice.

— Study your garden carefully and decide what you would like to highlight by the lighting.

— Ensure that the lighting professional has a copy of your landscape design.

— Include outdoor lighting while you are planning the landscape, as it will be easier to lay pipes and wires.

— Get more than one quotation so that you can compare prices.

— Install a transformer that is large enough to meet your current and future lighting needs.

— If you are planning to do part of the lighting now and the rest later on, then lay all the electrical groundwork in the first stage itself.

— Use soft light that looks like moonlight for the best results.

— Do not use too many lights; the landscape should be visible and not the lights.

— Hide the source of the lighting system behind plants and shrubs.

— The fixtures should not be visible, only the light from the bulbs should be seen.

— Use fixtures that are water resistant.

— Most people prefer using white light for landscapes, but with the help of a professional, you could try some color variation too.

— Use fluorescent lights are they are cheaper and more efficient that incandescent lights.

Outdoor Glass Lights

Outdoor lighting can highlight and add to the exterior of the house. Especially if glass lights are used outside the house it enhances the effects created by the lights. A wide variety of glass is used to make outdoor lights. Depending on the type of the glass used the appearance of the exterior can change. Here are a few types of glass that can be used for outdoor lighting:

— Blowing the glass around a mold and then passing it through an optic box creates the hammered look in hammered glass. Sandblasting can get the same effect.

— When air bubbles or particles are trapped in glass it is called seedy glass. This glass diffuses light in a beautiful manner.

— Once the glass is molded it is passed through rollers and the effect created on hardened glass is like waves. This is called water glass.

— Tiffany-Style or Mission-Style Glass is colored glass in different attractive pattern that can be used both indoors and outdoors.

— Alabaster glass is molded to look like alabaster marble. As a result the light is diffused and dim creating an ambience that is simple and beautiful.

— Glass that is either coated or sandblasted is called frosted glass. This is commonly used in modern fixtures. When this glass is used in lights it produces largely, even radiance.

Study Lights

Many of like to settle down comfortably in some favorite corner of the house and spend some time reading books or magazines we love. All of us have some reading and writing to do at some point of time. These two activities put a strain on our eyes and thus what is needed is proper lighting to reduce the strain. Adequate desk lighting is a must for students for long hours of night study. Here are a few tips on how the lighting should be while studying, writing or working on a computer:

— Lighting should be bright and must be focused on to the area where you are working.

— Use task lighting as it is focused and does not create any shadows. This lighting illuminates only the work surface like the study table.

— Use halogen bulbs as experts consider them the best to illuminate reading material.

— Using fluorescent bulbs is better than using incandescent bulbs. Fluorescent bulbs last longer, save electricity and are now available in a variety of colors.

— Right-handed individuals should place the light on their left hand side and vice versa. This is to ensure that the shadow of the hand does not fall the pages.

— You should sit upright and read with the material at a distance of about 14 to 18 inches away from the eyes.

— For long night study one should choose glare-free task lighting.

— As an individual grows older his eyes become weaker. Thus older people need more light for reading and writing.

Furnishing Hotels

Hotel furnishing is adding the final decorative touches to

your house to make it beautiful, elegant and stylish. It is while furnishing your hotel that you give it a distinctive look that is unique and is a reflection of your personality. Furnishing includes everything that you put into your hotel including furniture, the fabric for the curtains and cushions, the decorative items used to embellish your hotel etc. Some of the furnishing can be purely decorative or can be symbolic of something important to you or could be something that is of religious importance to you. The type of lighting used also influences the kind of style that you intend to create.

There are different types of hotel furnishing styles like cottage style, Victorian style, Mediterranean style, and modern style etc. It is best to read about all the styles and choose one that you are most comfortable with. The way you furnish your house should be according to the comfort level that it gives you and not based on what is fashionable at the moment. It is advisable to go through interior decoration magazines as well, as they give you a very good idea on how the various hotel furnishing styles actually look. After going through these magazines you may be able to find a style that suits you best. You could even combine various styles and create a new one to suit your needs.

Hotel furnishing and decoration should be done according to your budget. If you have the money then you can furnish your hotel using the best things available in the market. But you need not invest a lot of money in furnishing your hotel. You can furnish you hotel for less as well. By buying things at discount sales, wholesale stores and flea markets and using your imagination you can decorate your house elegantly. Always remember to use things you like. Your hotel should reflect your personality and you should feel comfortable in it.

Just the physical structure does not make a place hotel. It is what you put inside that structure and how it makes you feel and the mood it creates for you, that makes a cold building hotel. Furnishing an empty house seems like a daunting task. Many of us do not know how to go about furnishing a house and we do not know where to get furnishing ideas. Here are a few tips on how to furnish your house.

— The first thing you must do is to focus on what you like or dislike, whether it is style, fabric or colors.

— Decide on the style you want to use to furnish your house whether it is casual, traditional, French or modern.

— If you cannot make up your mind then buy a few interior decoration books. Go through them and you will be able to decide on a style that you like.

— The next step is to decide the colors you want to use to furnish your house. Choose colors that come to your mind when you say the word 'hotel'. Combine these colors to get more colors. Contrast and compliment the colors you like.

— Each room has a specific function from the user's point of view. Furnish the room depending on how you want to use it. For example you may want to use to kitchen as your dinning space as well. Then you will need to have a dinning table and chairs in the kitchen.

— A number of times the view that you get from your windows will dictate the way you furnish your house. If you can see the countryside from your window, then your interior décor and furnishing will match the country mood. If it is an urban cityscape that you can see from your window then your furnishing will be modern.

— Choose furniture that you are comfortable with. Do not go in for a particular style just because it is in vogue.

— You should be comfortable with the theme and the manner in which you have furnished your hotel. You should be able to relax and feel comfortable with the decorating you have done.

— Remember that your hotel should reflect your personality, taste and preferences and not someone else's.

When you begin, furnishing your hotel may seem like a difficult task, it is easy once you have decided what you like and what you dislike.

Cheap Furnishing

Furnishing your can be an expensive project. But you need not spend your entire savings on furnishing your house. Furnishing your can be an expensive project. But you need not spend your entire savings on furnishing your house. You need not hire an expensive interior decorator. Get ideas from magazines and use your own ideas and imagination to furnish your house. Before you invest in furnishing your house you must ask yourself for how long you plan to live in the house. Decide on the essential things that are required for furnishing your house and spend only on those. Look for places where you will get cheap deals, exclusive furnishings at discounted rates and furniture at discounts. Here are a few suggestions on where you are likely to get inexpensive furniture:

— Consignment stores where people sell used furniture.

— A developer's model hotel or sample flat in a pre-planned community may sell their furniture, when they need it no more.

— Warehouses of large furniture stores usually sell slightly damaged furniture and furniture that they have displayed for a while.

— Warehouses of wholesale furniture dealers may give you a discount on some of their pieces.

— If a neighbor in your locality is shifting he may want to dispose off his furniture and hold a yard sale. Keep a watch for yard sales.

— At the local flea market you can get decorative items for half their price. You can use these to decorate your house. When you go to the flea market, ensure that you go early, as the customers who come early get the best deals.

While furnishing your house remember that hotel furnishing should reflect your own unique style and personality. You should be comfortable in your hotel. This does not require expensive furnishing even with cheap hotel furnishing you can achieve the same style level. Use your imagination and creativity to furnish your hotel for less.

Hotel Furnishing Style

The first thing that you need to do, before you start furnishing your house, is to decide on a hotel furnishing style. Once you decide on a style it is easier to choose the furnishings and accessories that suit that style. Given below is a general overview of a few hotel furnishing styles, which you can consult before deciding on a particular style.

Cottage Style: The word cottage brings to mind a quaint little house, with a white picket fence, tucked away in the countryside or by a lake. For this style:

— Use white couches and chairs or white wicker furniture and for the cushions use floral prints.

— Paint the house in pastel shades.

— Use soft lighting and use dimmers if necessary.

— For curtains use sheer fabric or gauze. This will create the ambience of a cottage.

— Place antique accessories around the house.

— Use patchwork quilts as throws.

Mediterranean Style: This style of hotel furnishing is associated with the Italian and French styles.

— Use warm colors like earth colors or yellow.

— Use fabric with simple patterns in blue enhanced with a little gold.

— Use natural wood furniture.

— Decorate with pictures of flowers especially sunflower and ships.

Oriental Style: This style involves using simple and sleek Oriental patterns.

— While trying to create this style remember less is more.

— Use little furniture.

— Use tables made of teak wood and lacquer and coffee tables.

— Furnish with Oriental rugs, silk fabric with Oriental prints.

— Use pictures of dragons, cherry blossoms and Japanese seascapes.

Traditional Style: This style is the original classic hotel furnishing style, which is elegant but not loud.

— Use fabric with floral prints for curtains, cushions, couches, sheets etc.

— You can use plaids and damasks for furnishing as well.

— Use heavy material to make curtains.

— Use mahogany for furniture.

— Decorate with china, crystal.

— Used framed landscapes to decorate walls.

Hotel furnishing includes furniture, fabric for curtains, cushions etc. and hotel décor accessory. Accessories include works of art, wall hanging depicting landscapes or flowers or still life and decorative items that can be kept on the mantelpiece etc. It is these hotel décor accessories that add that special touch to your hotel and make it unique. Accessories reflect your personality and add a personal touch to the house. This decoration and arrangement of the interior that makes your hotel the most comfortable place on the surface of the earth. Here are a few suggestions on how you can decorate your house.

— Use artwork as hotel décor wall accessory. Artworks reflect your personality. Pictures of horizontal landscape widen room; floral pictures give an illusion of height, using such pictures will change the shape of the room if placed properly.

— While hanging small pictures cluster them together to create the image of a single unit and hang at eye level.

— Large pictures must be positioned in proportion to the furniture in the room and hang them at eye level.

— Carefully placed mirrors can create the illusion of space. In a dark room, hanging a decorative mirror near the window, ill allow the mirror to reflect the light from the window, thus lighting up the room.

— By using different types of lights you can create different moods in different rooms of the house.

— Use flowering pots to decorate your house. You can select flowers according to the color of the rest of the room.

— Flowers and potted plants add a natural touch to the house and make it more appealing.

— Using area rugs will add color and warmth to the room. Use contrasting colors on wooden floors and the room will come alive.

— Use cushions for a warm and cozy feeling in the house. Scatter them on the area rug; use them on couches, sofas and beds. Use cushion made of different material and in bright colors.

Follow these simple tips on how to use hotel décor accessory and you will have a warm and beautiful hotel.

How to Buy Carpet

A carpet is an essential item while furnishing your hotel. Selecting a carpet is not an easy task, as there is a wide variety to choose from and the price range is just as extensive. Many of us do not know how to buy a carpet and the things that we should look for while buying a carpet. An important thing to remember is that the more expensive the carpet the better the quality of the carpet. Therefore buy the best you can afford. Here are a few tips to keep in mind while buying a carpet.

Construction of Carpet: The construction of tufted carpets falls into one of the following types and all carpets are a variation of one of these constructions.

— *Cut Pile:* The woven loops are cut and a result the carpet has single, individual tips. This carpet can be used in any part of the house.

— *Loop Pile:* The surface of the carpet is made of loops. These carpets are very durable and should be used in areas that are frequently used.

— *Cut and Loop Pile:* These carpets are a blend of cut and loop pile in various design. This type of carpet in bright colors is very good at hiding dirt and soil.

Fibers. Carpets are made from different types of fibers and each has its own advantages and disadvantages.

— *Nylon*: this is the most commonly used fiber for carpets. If it get stained it can be cleaned easily.

— *Polyester:* Carpets made of polyester are extremely soft and the colors show up very well in this fiber. It does not stain and fade easily and is cheaper than nylon.

— *Polypropylene (Olefin):* This is a very popular fiber for carpets as it resistant to stains, fading and water and it is inexpensive.

— *Wool:* A carpet made of wool is lavish do doubt but it is the most expensive.

Face Weight: Face weight is the number of ounces of fiber per square yard of carpet. Usually a carpet with greater face weight is of a better quality.

Fiber Density: Fiber density is how closely carpet fiber or yarn is pilled together and tied into the carpet backing. If a carpet has high fiber density then the carpet will look more luxurious and feel more comfortable under your feet.

Twist and Tuft Bind: Twist is the number of times fiber strands are twisted together in an inch length of carpet yarn. The twist affects the texture and appearance of cut pile carpet. Normally greater the number of twists per inch length of carpet yarn more durable the carpet.Tuft bind is the relative strength of the loop yarn attached to the backing of the carpet. Greater the number of tuft binds better the quality of the carpet.

Padding: A well-padded carpet will last longer than a poorly padded one. Padding makes the carpet more comfortable to walk on. Thin, firm pads are better than thick, soft pads. Normally carpet width is either 12' or 15' wide. If you want to carpet a large room you may have to sew together carpets.

Selecting Artwork

When you move into your new house, the most exciting thing is to decorate the house, to make it the house of your dreams. While decorating you will decorate the walls of the house you would like to make them look beautiful but unique. One way of decorating the walls is to hang works of art on the walls. You can either buy originals or reproductions depending on your budget. Selecting art for your house is not an easy task. Here are a few pointers on selecting art for your hotel.

- Art works make a statement about the kind of person you are. So when you select art it should be because you love it and not because it matches your sofa or carpet.
- Art should be bought for its own value and nothing else.
- Buy art that you can enjoy for a long time. Buy something that you will not get bored of in a short time.
- The artwork should create the mood of the room and everything in the room should compliment it and not the other way round.
- You will be attracted to artwork that seem to perfectly fit your hotel and to colors and themes that interest you. If your house is decorated in a traditional fashion then you will be attracted to traditional paintings. If it is decorated in a contemporary style you will be attracted to contemporary paintings.
- By talking to the owners of art galleries and interior decorators you can get suggestions on how to select and appreciate artwork.

8

Budget Preparation

All housekeeping managers are responsible for ensuring that the resources of their program are used responsibly and appropriately. Every manager needs to be skilled in financial management because an important part of any manager's job is planning, monitoring, recording, and controlling the financial resources which are used to get the work done.

Financial management means managing an organization's resources to meet organizational goals and objectives as effectively as possible by using those resources to carry out planned activities. Financial management also ensures that there are adequate resources available to carry out the activities which have been outlined by the organization during the planning process.

Most hospitality organizations are nonprofit and define their goals and objectives in terms of services they provide to a community. These service objectives are usually determined periodically during the planning of the program. Once the goals and objectives have been set, the tools and techniques of financial management are used to ensure that adequate funds are available to achieve these planned objectives in the most cost-effective way.

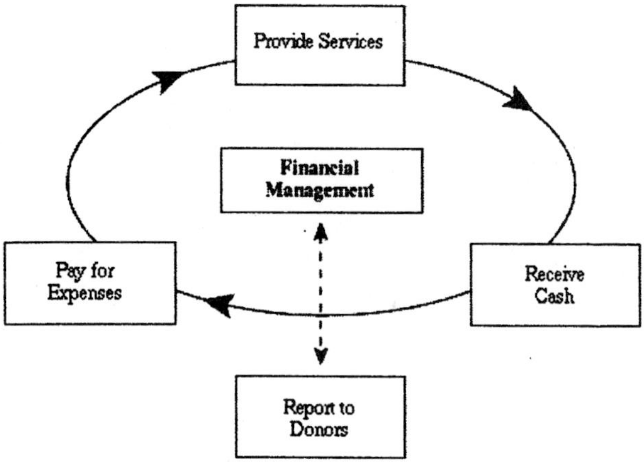

The financial management cycle

The planning process serves to define service objectives and describe the activities necessary to achieve them. The expenses that are incurred in carrying out these activities are then financed either by the services that are being provided or by outside sources. The financial management cycle therefore consists of providing services, receiving cash, paying for expenses, and reporting to donors and other outside sources on the use of funds that have been provided.

Financial Management Skills

As manager of a housekeeping, you will need to know enough about financial principles to be capable of:

— Preparing a budget for your work plan;

— Projecting revenues and monitoring cash flow;

— Controlling and managing funds (establishing basic standards and controls);

— Financial monitoring (comparing program results with budget projections);

— Determining and comparing the cost of services;
— Meeting both donor and institutional reporting requirements;
— Understanding and using financial reports for decision making.

These topics will be described in the following pages. They have been singled out in this handbook because many housekeeping managers are being challenged to:

— Maintain or expand services in the face of reduced funding from donors or governments;
— Institute alternative financing of f housekeeping services, which requires the development of multi-level financial management controls;
— Compare the effectiveness of different service approaches or sites within the system, which require the development of ways to measure the cost of f housekeeping services;
— Meet the different reporting and procedural requirements of multiple funding sources.

The financial duties of managers in the public and private sector differ. In the public sector, most housekeeping managers are given a fixed budget allocation. If their allocation is not sufficient, their only choices are to try and obtain an increase or to cut expenses. Often, their ability to make these adjustments is restricted, as they have limited knowledge of personnel costs, and civil service regulations give them little control over the hiring and firing of staff. Furthermore, they may be working within a set system of accounting standards, financial controls, and informational reports that they can do little to change. However, in many ministries, financial systems are becoming more decentralized, and their is increasing interest in charging fees for services to cover at least part of the cost incurred by the program. As a result, increasing numbers of public sector managers face financial management tasks that were formerly limited to the private sector, such as studying the cost-effectiveness of their clinic-based versus community-based services.

Cost management

There is an inherent problem in the study of cost control or, more accurately, cost management. The simple fact is that management's primary responsibility is to deliver a quality product or service to the guest, at a price mutually agreeable to both parties. In addition, the quality must be such that the consumer, or end user of the product or service, feels that excellent value was received for the money spent on the transaction. When this level of service is achieved, the business will prosper. If management focuses on controlling costs more than servicing guests, problems will certainly surface.

It is important to remember that guests cause businesses to incur costs. You do not want to get yourself in the mind-set of reducing costs to the point where it is thought that "low" costs are good and "high" costs are bad. If there are fewer guests, there are likely to be fewer costs, but fewer profits as well! Because that is true, when management attempts to reduce costs, with no regard for the impact on the balance between managing costs and guest satisfaction, the business will surely suffer. In addition, efforts to reduce costs that result in unsafe conditions for guests or employees are never wise. While some shortterm savings may result, the expense of a lawsuit resulting from a guest or employee injury can be very high. Managers who, for example, neglect to spend the money to salt and shovel a snowy restaurant entrance area may find that they spend thousands more dollars defending themselves in a lawsuit brought by an individual who slipped and fell on the ice.

As an effective housekeeping manager, the question to be considered is not whether costs are high or low. The question is whether costs are too high or too low, given management's view of the value it hopes to deliver to the guest and the goals of the housekeeping operation's owners. Managers can eliminate nearly all costs by closing the operation's doors. Obviously, however, when you close the doors to expense, you close the doors to profits. Expenses, then, must be incurred, and they must be managed in a way that allows the operation to achieve its desired profit levels. As a housekeeping operator, you must realize that the difference between what you have paid for the goods you sell and the price at which you sell them does not represent your actual profit. Instead, all expenses, including advertising, the building housing your operation, management salaries, and the labor required to generate the sale, to name but a few, are expenses that must be subtracted before you can determine your profits accurately.

Every housekeeping operator is faced with the following profit-oriented formula:

$$\text{Revenue} - \text{Expenses} = \text{Profit}$$

Thus, when you manage your facility, you will receive revenue, the money you take in, and you will incur expenses, the cost of the items required to operate the business. The dollars that remain after all expenses have been paid represent your profit. Here, we will use the following terms interchangeably: revenues and sales; expenses and costs.

In your own operation, if you find that revenue is less than or equal to real expense, with no reserve for the future, you will likely also find that there is no money for new equipment; needed equipment maintenance may not be performed; employee raises may be few and far between; and, in general, the hotel will become outdated due to a lack of funds needed to remodel and upgrade. The truth is, all hotels need revenue in excess of expenses if they are to thrive. If you manage a housekeeping operation in a profit or a nonprofit setting, it will be your responsibility to communicate this message to your own staff.

Profit is the result of solid planning, sound management, and careful decision making. The purpose of this text is to give you the information and tools you need to make informed decisions with regard to managing your operation's revenue and expenses. If these tools are utilized properly, the potential for achieving profits you desire is greatly enhanced.

Profit should not be viewed as what is left over after the bills are paid. In fact, careful planning is necessary to earn a profit. In most cases, investors will not invest in businesses that do not generate enough profit to make their investment worthwhile. The restaurant business can be very profitable; however, there is no guarantee that an individual restaurant will in fact make a profit. Some restaurants do, while others do not. Because that is true, a more appropriate formula, which recognizes and rewards the business owner for the risk associated with business ownership or investment, is as follows:

$$\text{Revenue} - \text{Desired Profit} = \text{Ideal Expense}$$

Ideal expense, in this case, is defined as management's view of the correct or appropriate amount of expense necessary to generate a given quantity of revenue. Desired profit is defined as the profit that the owner wants to achieve on that predicted quantity of revenue. This formula clearly places profit as a reward for providing service, not a leftover. When housekeeping managers deliver quality and value to their guests, anticipated revenue levels can be achieved and desired profit is attainable. Desired profit and ideal expense levels are not, however, easily achieved. It takes an astute housekeeping operator to consistently make decisions that will maximize revenue while holding expenses to the ideal or appropriate amount.

Revenue

To some degree, you can manage your revenue levels. Revenue dollars are the result of units sold. These units may consist of individual menu items, lunches, dinners, drinks, or any other item produced by your operation. Revenue varies with both the number of guests frequenting your business and the amount of money spent by each guest. You can increase revenue by increasing the number of guests you serve, by increasing the amount each guest spends, or by a combination of both approaches. Adding seating or drive-through windows and extending operating hours are all examples of management's efforts to increase the number of guests choosing to come to your hotel.

Experienced housekeeping operators know that increasing revenue through adding guests, suggestive selling, or possibly raising menu prices is an extremely effective way of increasing overall profitability, but only if effective cost management systems are in place. The focus of this chapter is on managing and controlling expenses, not generating additional revenue. While the two topics are clearly related, they are different. Marketing efforts, hotel design and site selection and employee training are all critical links in the revenue-producing chain. No amount of effective expense control can solve the profit problems caused by inadequate revenue resulting from inferior quality or service levels. Effective cost control, however, when coupled with management's aggressive attitude toward meeting and exceeding guests' expectations, can result in outstanding revenue and profit performance.

Percent Review

Understanding percents and how they are mathematically computed is important. The following review may be helpful for some readers. If you thoroughly understand the percent concept, you may skip this section and the Computing Percent section and proceed directly to the Using Percent section. Percent (%) means "out of each hundred." Thus, 10 percent would mean 10 out of each 100. If we asked how many guests would buy blueberry pie on a given day, and the answer is 10 percent, then 10 people out of each 100 we serve will select blueberry pie. If 52 percent of your employees are female, then 52 out of each 100 employees are female. If 15 percent of your employees will receive a raise this month, then 15 out of 100 employees will get their raise.

In its common form, the % sign is used to express the percentage. If we say 10 percent, then we mean "10 out of each 100" and no further explanation is necessary. The common form, the percent, is equivalent to the same amount expressed in either the fraction or the decimal form.

In fraction form, the percent is expressed as the part, or a portion of 100. Thus, 10 percent is written as 10 "over" 100 (10/100). This is simply another way of expressing the relationship between the part (10) and the whole (100).

A decimal is a number developed from the counting system we use. It is based on the fact that we count to 10 then start over again. In other words, each of our major units, 10s, 100s, 1,000s, and so on, are based on the use of

10s, and each number can easily be divided by 10. Instead of using the % sign, the decimal form uses the (.) or decimal point to express the percent relationship. Thus, 10 percent is expressed as 0.10 in decimal form. The numbers to the right of the decimal point express the percentage.

Each of these three methods of expressing percentages is used in the hotel industry, and to be successful you must develop a clear understanding of how a percentage is computed. Once that is known, you can express the percentage in any form that is required or that is useful to you.

To determine what percent one number is of another number, divide the number that is the part by the number that is the whole. Usually, but not always, this means dividing the smaller number by the larger number. For example, assume that 840 guests were served during a banquet at your hotel; 420 of them asked for coffee with their meal. To find what percent of your guests ordered coffee, divide the part (420) by the whole (840).

The process looks as follows:

$$\frac{\text{part}}{\text{whole}} = \text{percent or } \frac{420}{840} = 0.50$$

Thus, 50% (common form), 50/100 (fraction form), or 0.50 (decimal form) represents the proportion of people at the banquet who ordered coffee. A large number of new housekeeping managers have difficulty computing percent figures. It is easy to forget which number goes "on the top" and which number goes "on the bottom." In general, if you attempt to compute a percentage and get a whole number (a number larger than 1), either a mistake has been made or costs are extremely high! Many people also become confused when converting from one form of percent to another. If that is a problem, remember the following conversion rules:

1. To convert from common form to decimal form, move the decimal two places to the left, that is, 50.00% _ 0.50.
2. To convert from decimal form to common form, move the decimal two places to the right, that is, 0.40 _ 40.00%.

In a hotel, the "whole" is usually a revenue figure. Expenses and profits are the "parts," which are usually expressed in terms of a percent. It is interesting to note that, in the United States, the same system in use for our numbers is in use for our money. Each dime contains 10 pennies, each dollar contains 10 dimes, and so on. Thus when discussing money, it is true that a percent refers to "cents out of each dollar" as well as "out of each 100 dollars." When we say 10 percent of a dollar, we mean 10 cents, or "10 cents out of each dollar." Likewise, 25 percent of a dollar represents 25 cents, 50 percent of a dollar represents 50 cents, and 100 percent of a dollar represents $1.00.

Sometimes, when using percent to express the relationship between portions of a dollar and the whole, we find that the part is, indeed, larger than the whole. Great care must always be taken when computing percents, so that the percent arrived at is of help to you in your work and does not represent an error in mathematics.

Profit and Loss Statement

An accounting tool that details revenue, expenses, and profit for a given period of time, is called the income statement, which is commonly called the profitand-loss statement (P&L). The P&L also identifies profits since, as you recall, profits are generated by the formula:

Revenue – Expense = Profit

The P&L is important because it indicates the efficiency and profitability of an operation. Because so many individuals and groups are interested in a hotel's performance, it is important that the P&L and other financial statements are prepared in a manner that is consistent with other facilities. If, for example, you own two Italian restaurants, it would be very confusing if one of your managers used a particular method for preparing his or her unit's P&L, while the other manager used an entirely different method. You, your investors, your accountant, governmental taxing entities, and your creditors may all be interested in your operational results, and unless you report and account for these in a manner they can easily understand, confusion may result.

To avoid such a set of circumstances, the Uniform System of Accounts is used to report financial results in most hotels. This system was created to ensure uniform reporting of financial results. A Uniform System of Accounts exists for restaurants, another for hotels, and another for clubs. The Uniform System of Accounts will be discussed in greater detail later in this text. The primary purpose of preparing a P&L is to identify revenue, expenses, and profits for a given time period. As a manager, your efforts, more than any other factor, will influence your operation's profitability.

Good managers provide excellent value to their guests, which cause guests to return, and thus increases revenue. In addition, good managers know how to analyze, manage, and control their costs. For these managers, expenses are held to the amount that was preplanned. The result is the desired profit level. Good managers influence the success of their units and their own employees. The results for them personally are promotions, added responsibilities, and salary increases. If you wish to succeed in the hospitality industry, it is important to remember that your performance will be evaluated primarily on your ability to achieve the profit levels your operation has planned for.

All effective managers, whether in the commercial (for profit) or nonprofit sector, use budgets. Budgeting is simply planning for revenue, expense, and profit. If these items are planned for, you can determine how close your actual performance is to your plan or budget.

UNDERSATNDING THE BUDGET

A simple example may help to firmly establish the idea of budget and performance to budget. Assume that a child has $1.00 per day to spend on candy. On Monday morning, the child's parents give the child $1.00 for each day of the week, or $7.00 total. If the child spends only $ 1.00 per day, he or she will be able to buy candy all week. If, however, too much is spent in any one day, there may not be any money left at the end of the week. Too ensure a week of candy eating, a good "candy purchasing" pattern could be created,. The "% of Total" column is computed by dividing $1.00 (the part) by $7.00 (the whole). Notice that we can determine the percent of total that should have been spent by any given day; that is, each day equals 14.28 percent, or 1/7 of the total.

Many hotels are changing from "one month" budget periods to periods of 28 days. The 28-day-period approach divides a year into 13 equal periods of 28 days each. Therefore, each period has four Mondays, four Tuesdays, four Wednesdays, and so on. This helps the manager compare performance from one period to the next without having to compensate for "extra days" in any one period. The downside of this approach is that you can no longer talk about the month of March, for example, because "period 3" would occur during part of February and part of March. Although using the 28-day-period approach takes a while to get used to, it is an effective way to measure performance and plan from period to period.

We can use the expense records from the previous summer as well as our solid industry knowledge and experience to develop expense budget figures for this summer. In this case, we are interested in both our plan (budget) and our actual performance.

Many operators use the concept of "significant" variation to determine whether a cost control problem exists. In this case, a significant variation is any variation in expected costs that management feels is an area of concern. This variation can be caused by costs that were either higher or lower than the amount originally budgeted or planned for.

When you manage a housekeeping operation and you find that significant variations from your planned results occur, you must:

1. Identify the problem.
2. Determine the cause.
3. Take corrective action.

It is crucial to know the kind of problem you have if you are to be an effective problem solver. Management's attention must be focused on the proper place. In this case, the proper areas for concern are other expense and profit. If, in the future, expenses became too low, it, too, would be an area of concern. Why? Remember that expenses create revenue; thus, it is not your goal to eliminate expense. In fact, those managers who focus too much on eliminating expense, instead of building revenue, often find that their expenses are completely eliminated when they are forced to close their operation's doors permanently because guests did not feel they received good value for the money spent at that restaurant! Control and management of revenue and expense are important. Elimination of either is not desired. As you have seen, revenue and expense directly impact profit. Your important role as a hospitality manager is to analyze, manage, and control your costs so that you achieve planned results. It can be done, and it can be fun. The remainder of this text discusses how you can best manage and account for revenue and expense. With a good understanding of the relationship among revenue, expense, and profit, and your ability to analyze using percentages, you are ready to begin the cost control and cost management process.

Preparing a Budget

All budgets itemize the costs that are expected to be incurred by a set of activities; most budgets also specify the income that is expected to cover these costs. A budget can be drawn up for a single activity, such as a training workshop, or for a whole program or organization. A program or organization should use the operating budgets of all its internal operating centers in developing its own operating budget. An operating budget is based on the year's work plan and on information about centralized costs. It itemizes the cost for one year of carrying out all activities and the expected income that they will pay for them.

Just as the work plan is based on the long-term plans, the budget also relates to the financial plan and thus reflects the financial aspects of the long-term plan.

Budgeting is important because:

— The exercise of preparing a budget forces managers to think each activity through in detail and commit their thoughts to paper;

— Budgets give managers essential information on the projected expenses and income associated with planned activities; this information lets managers know whether all planned activities are financially feasible and whether more income needs to be raised or costs need to be reduced;

— When developed in accordance with work plans, budgets help managers to ensure that organizational resources are spent only on planned activities;

— The planner is forced to differentiate between essential and non-essential activities and to give essential activities a higher priority;

— By listing in detail the projected expenses and the expected funding sources, budgets help the organization to prepare to secure the resources needed to meet these expenses;

— Budgets allow managers to evaluate the actual costs of activities and thus to consider alternatives if the planned activities are too costly;

— By having a realistic, updated budget and comparing it with actual expenses, managers can be forewarned of potential shortfalls in the resources that are available for specific activities

There are two basic steps to preparing a budget: identifying necessary resources and their costs, and determining their sources of funding.

The first step is to specify all the resources that are needed to implement the activities listed in the work plan and to assign a cost to these resources. To do this, look at each activity in the work plan and quantify the time, supplies, equipment, and other costs required to carry it out.

Most of the costs of your activities will be variable costs. These are costs that vary with the volume of service or scope of activities that you will provide. Some costs, however, will be "fixed." Fixed costs are incurred by the program no matter what the level of activity or volume of service is. Examples of fixed costs are rent and utilities, equipment leases or payments, and most salaries. Both variable and fixed costs must be included in your budget.

The second step in budget preparation is to determine where the resources you need will come from and which expenses will be paid for by which funding source. For many public programs, this step is simple because there is only one funding source, the government. But in private programs or in public programs that receive private money or charge fees to generate income, the task of identifying ways to finance activities is more complex.

Monitoring Cash Flow

Managers must ensure that they have adequate cash in the bank or funds in their allocation to cover all anticipated financial obligations each month. The first step in this management task is to project, during the planning process, the cash flow and the funding availability. Once the work plan and budget are completed, the manager uses both documents to analyze the timing of anticipated expenditures. By comparing these with the timing of anticipated receipts, the manager can see whether there are any periods in which there will be insufficient funds.

Strategies for Anticipated Cash Shortages

There are three basic strategies for dealing with periods in which you foresee insufficient funds. As a manager, you should find that at least one of these strategies is feasible for your program.

- — Adjust the timing of activities in the work plan, or cut other expenses from the budget;
- — Rearrange a donor or ministry payment schedule so that large payments precede large expenditures;
- — Arrange for a short-term loan.

Failure to predict cash flow accurately can cause cash shortages at crucial moments in the life of a program, leading to delays in the payment of salaries, inability to buy basic supplies when needed, and other emergencies, all of which result in the program's failure to achieve its objectives.

Develop a Cash Flow Projections Worksheet

The cash flow projections worksheet is a key monitoring tool that can help a manager anticipate the amount of cash needed to cover anticipated expenditures. By projecting revenues and expenses, the worksheet shows the inflows and outflows of cash that are anticipated during a specific period of time. A manager can use the worksheet to compare actual revenues and expenditures with those which were projected, in order to ensure that sufficient funds are available at all times to meet program needs.

Controlling and Managing Funds

Good financial control procedures and a sound accounting system are the foundation for effective financial management. While financial managers or bookkeepers are responsible for setting up and maintaining an accounting and financial control system, the general manager bears the ultimate responsibility for a program and must know enough about the system to supervise both bookkeepers and financial managers.

Accounting standards and financial management controls are the procedures, guidelines, and rules that help to ensure that:

— Funds and resources are used responsibly and appropriately

— The financial information provides a complete and accurate picture of the inflows and outflows of resources and cash

Specifically, financial controls ensure that:

— Receipts and disbursements are handled according to authorized procedures;

— Transactions are properly recorded so that the organization can account for its assets and prepare accurate and comprehensive financial statements;

— Access to assets is permitted only with authorization by the appropriate manager;

— Assets are physically checked at regular intervals (inventory) and appropriate action is taken when there are differences between the records and the physical count.

Requirements for Effective Financial management

The two main principles for an effective financial control system are:

Duties are divided among individuals in such a way that no one person can control all the phases of a transaction. For example:

— One single employee cannot request, approve, and make payments

— Bank account reconciliations are done by an employee who doesn't sign checks, has no access to cash, and doesn't record cash transactions

— Financial records are reviewed periodically by a responsible person other than the person who normally maintains the records.

— The person controlling commodities, equipment, and supplies is not responsible for purchase and receipt of these items

— The person distributing salary cash or checks should not be the same person who calculates and prepares the payroll

Auditing your program

Accounting and financial control procedures regulate transactions as they occur in the system. For example:

— All inflows and outflows of cash or resources are documented.

— Pre-printed, serially numbered receipts and payment vouchers are used.

— Monthly bank account reconciliations are performed, and any discrepancies found are investigated.

— Time and attendance records are kept for all employees.

— When payments are made with cash rather than a check, petty cash vouchers and receipts must be submitted.

— Deposits of cash sales or fees are made frequently.

— All grant payments must be approved in writing by the director.

— All purchases are approved before an order is placed.

Having an annual external audit is an important way for you as a manager to know whether controls and procedures are operating properly. However, it is important for the institutional audit to cover both the donor funds and the organization's own funds, so that it gives a complete picture. Audits of individual donor funds should be discouraged since they do not provide a complete picture. Instead, it is better to have donors help pay for an institutional audit.

Authorizing Purchases

Some non-financial managers, particularly those in smaller organizations or in charge of service sites, have the responsibility of authorizing expenditures and purchases. How can they ensure that:

— The purchase is justified

— The cost is competitive

— The transaction is properly documented

— There are sufficient funds to make the purchase?

To ensure that a purchase is justified, the manager institutes a voucher or purchase order system, whereby purchases must be pre-approved before any checks or cash are disbursed. As a criterion for approval, the manager or financial officer can check to see whether or not the item appears in the budget and can request documentation for purchases that had not been anticipated.

To ensure that the cost is competitive, the manager can make sure that at least three suppliers (when available) were contacted in order to make price comparisons. In the case of supplies or a piece of equipment, it often suffices to compare prices in catalogs or through phone calls. For larger expenditures, such as a printing job or construction, it is customary to solicit bids or written estimates and to use the contractor that offers the lowest bid along with acceptable quality of work.

To ensure that the transaction is properly documented, all checks and pre-printed, serially numbered cash receipts bear the corresponding purchase order number.

To ensure that there are sufficient funds to cover the purchase, the manager can check the budget performance report and the cash flow report, which monitor actual expenses and expenditures, against the budget in order to see whether a particular category is being overspent, or whether the whole budget is overspent, thus necessitating cutbacks in all categories. The budget performance report should also monitor the actual receipt of revenues against those projected in the budget and cash flow forecast, as well as whether these revenues are government allocations, service-generated revenues, or grants. If the timing of receipts is delayed, or if generated income is lower than expected, there may not be enough funds to cover a large purchase.

Managing Small Amounts

Many managers, particularly those operating housekeeping service sites, are responsible for managing cash. They may be responsible for petty cash funds; some discretionary funds for programs; funds for training, transportation, and small purchases; and cash generated by payment for services or sales of contraceptives.

Monitoring Finances

When overseeing an organization's finances, a key monitoring task is to compare the actual revenues and expenses with those which were projected in the budget. This information is crucial. Most managers need to take immediate action when revenue is lower or expenses are higher than projected in the budget. Furthermore, you cannot prepare a realistic budget for the next year without comparing this year's budget with the actual results.

Financial monitoring can only be done well by working as a team with your financial manager and by looking at planning and monitoring as unified parts of the same cycle. Both financial and program managers must:

— Project expenses and revenues during the planning process.

— Compare actual revenues and expenses with projections while monitoring the project.

The financial planning and monitoring cycle usually works as follows:

— The program and financial managers work together to determine the key planning and monitoring information that is needed from the financial information system.

— The program and financial managers develop the structure of the chart of accounts, the budget, and the financial reports.

— During the planning process, the program managers develop a budget that projects the next year's revenues and expenses.

— The financial managers oversee the accounting system that records the expenses incurred and the revenues generated during the program implementation.

— The financial managers and /or accounting staff generate the needed reports from the accounting system at regular intervals during the program's implementation.

— Financial and program managers discuss any shortfalls or excess in revenues or expenses and determine whether any adjustments are needed in program or management activities.
— Financial and program managers use the financial reports to plan for the next year's budget.

Determining the Cost of Services

Through a system of cost accounting, the manager can determine the actual costs of a particular service, service facility, or program. The cost of individual facilities in programs also includes some share of the indirect costs of the larger programs, but it is a challenge to determine how large that share should be. This information is useful for several purposes:

In services that are trying to recover costs through charging fees, cost information is essential in order to set prices.

— When the manager wants to compare the cost and effectiveness of different facilities, providers, or service strategies, cost information is an essential basis for this comparison.
— In a cost accounting system, the basic challenge is the integration of cost information with program information.

Integrating Cost Information with Program Information

In housekeeping programs, there are three common obstacles to overcome in order to generate accurate cost information for the purpose of measuring cost-effectiveness or of setting fees:

— *Tracking resources used in cash-based accounting systems.* Housekeeping programs typically use the cash-based accounting system. Cash-based systems record resources purchased rather than resources used. For example, if two years' worth of supplies are brought in Year One, analyzing costs on a cash basis alone will inflate the supplies' cost for the first year. Furthermore, the cost of donated assets and costs associated with the deprecation of fixed assets are often not recorded.

A modified cash-based system keeps track of receivables (money you have earned but not yet received), payables (money that you owe), depreciation, and contraceptive/medical supplies used. The latter can be tracked through conducting regular inventory of supplies.

— *Separating housekeeping costs from the costs of other services.* When housekeeping services are integrated with other social services, the financial information does not separate housekeeping costs from the costs of these other services.

— *Calculating indirect costs.* If the manager wishes to compare the cost-effectiveness of different operating centers or projects, the financial information does not record the indirect costs of running an operating center within a program. For example, usually some of the administrative costs of running an operating center are incurred in a central or regional office.

The cost study must estimate what percentage of the administrative costs of the total program corresponds to the costs of running any one project or operating center within the program. One method that a manager might use to make this estimate is the cost method. To use this method, take the cost of one operating center and divide it by the total cost of all of the operating centers within the program. For example, if the annual budget of Clinic A is $10,000,

> and the annual budgets of all ten clinics in the program amount to $100,000, then the costs of Clinic A are 10 percent of the direct costs of the program, and 10 percent of the costs of the central office could logically be assigned to Clinic A.

A program that strives for excellence will always use some measure to evaluate the success of different strategies or service sites within the program. In most fields, success is a relative concept and is measured by comparing similar programs or service sites to see which is most or least successful. The manager will have to decide whether to drop or alter those programs which are found to be the least successful, as well as whether the most successful can be reproduced. This process allows the manager to make the best use of the available resources.

Cost-effectiveness studies enable the manager to make these comparisons by using quantitative measures of results that are used by all of the programs or services being studied. These studies can be used in conjunction with qualitative measures of program performance to make program decisions. For example, the cost per user of a rural service might be higher than that of a more centralized service site, but the manager might decide to put additional resources into the rural site for political reasons or because the contraceptive prevalence is unusually high for that area.

To perform a cost-effectiveness analysis, you must be able to:

— Assign costs to the service you are trying to assess;

— Choose a quantifiable output or result of the program that can serve as a key measure of the program's effectiveness or success;

— Identify the cost per output or result.

Meeting Reporting Requirements

Managers are asked to meet the reporting requirements of their own institutions as well as those of the institutions that support them. Often these requirements are different and require an organization to develop a system that is flexible enough to satisfy these numerous requirements without additional time and effort.

Programs or projects may have separate sources of funds, as well as separate planning and budgetary processes. Managers may be required both to consolidate financial information to determine the overall financial picture of the organization and to account separately for activities financed by different funding sources.

It is important to strike a balance between your internal information needs and the reporting requirements of donors. Failure to consider your organization's internal needs as well as the needs of the donor can lead to the following situations:

— In a decentralized management system, where lower-level managers are involved in financial planning, budgeting, controlling and reporting, it is vital that they be able to get financial information at their level. Many organizations have difficulty providing reports at this level when their financial information systems are donor-driven.

— Many organizations with several donors have a separate project budget for each donor, each covering several years, but have no consolidated information or financial plan to allow them to make organization-wide strategic decisions.

To create a system that meets both the needs of your organization and those of your funding institution, it is helpful to:

Negotiate with donors. Donors demand a great many detailed financial reports that often do not correspond to either the needs of the organization or its reporting periods. In order to make it easier to prepare a consolidated financial plan, you can try to negotiate with donors so that their projects cover logical portions of the plan. For example, it can be confusing when one person's time or the costs for one operating center, such as a clinic, are being paid for by several donors. It is useful to organize donor "projects" so that they correspond to the operating centers that you have set up in your accounting system. It is also useful to try to negotiate donor reporting periods that fit in with your existing system.

Sort information by funding source and operating center. The basis for developing a unified planning and reporting system budget is an accounting system, which allocates expenses to both operating centers and sources of funding. In a computerized system, putting your financial information in a database simplifies this task. One field allows you to sort expenses and revenues by operating center, while another field allows you to sort them by funding source.

It is still possible, but more time-consuming, to organize your financial information by donor or source of revenue in a non-computerized system, by developing a numbering code for each possible source. When recording expenses, one column in the journal could be titled "account charged." Besides each expense, your bookkeeper will be able to put a number in this column for the project or grant to which this is charged. In programs that generate revenues from sales or unrestricted donations, there will always be one code for "unrestricted." In order to collect the expense information for each source of revenue into one report, the bookkeeper will have to collect it manually by reviewing each expense account and selecting those marked with the appropriate code.

Another way to produce reports on expenses by source is to have a separate set of accounting journals for each project or funding source. When the accounting system is organized this way, however, it becomes a challenge to produce financial information for the whole organization or program.

Recording revenues by source is easier for the accounting system to handle, since each source will have a separate journal or account.

Donors generally have differing financial reporting formats and reporting periods, which complicates the tasks of accounting and reporting. The most common problems and possible solutions are as follows:

— *Donors have different reporting periods.* Some require reports every three months, some every four months, while often none of these may correspond to your organization's fiscal year.Your information may need to be organized by month, so that differing reporting periods can be handled by your system.

— *Variations in donor requirements create inconsistencies in the categories under which certain line items fall.* For example, some donors require office supplies to be shown under "Administrative Expenses," and other donors wish it to be shown under "Supplies" together with contraceptives. A computerized sorting system is often the only way to deal with conflicting categorization of criteria for different funders.

Using Financial Reports for Decision-Making

Financial reports are the main product of this financial information system, and as such they are crucial to your ability to monitor your program. Your whole financial information system, from the chart of accounts and the budget to the financial reports, should be tailored to fit your specific needs for monitoring information as a manager in your own unique context.

The design of all elements of the system can and should be reviewed regularly, because as your environment changes, your needs for financial information will change: a new donor will have different reporting requirements, or your program will begin to charge fees for the first time, or new activities will require the creation of new budget line items. Your system will need to be flexible enough to incorporate these changes.

Different types of housekeeping programs have very different financial monitoring needs. Most public sector managers only use expenditure reports to compare actual expenditures with their budget; the reports are rarely used for any cost accounting or cost-effectiveness analysis, such as analyzing the cost per unit of service.

The Balance Sheet

A balance sheet is designed to show the financial position of an organization at a particular point in time. It shows the assets, liabilities, and reserves. It is called a balance sheet because it must "balance," that is, the liabilities subtracted from the assets must equal the reserves. A balance sheet is used to assess the financial structure and stability of an organization, for example, to see whether its liabilities can be met. "Reserves" can be defined as the financial value of the organization after the liabilities are settled. In a commercial organization, this is generally the equity - the value of the owner's investment plus accumulated profits or income. In a nonprofit organization, this represents the institutional "fund balance."

The income statement

An income statement is designed to show the income (profit) or deficit (loss) of an organization during a specific period of time. It shows the revenues minus the expenses and the resulting profit or loss. The income statement is used to assess the overall financial performance of the organization as well as the relative performance of departments. It is also used to compare actual with budgeted income and expenditures, in order to monitor the budgetary performance and to identify where budgets need to be revised or action needs to be taken to modify activities, reduce costs, or change prices.

For programs that generate income from sales of goods or services, the monthly sales report is an essential monitoring document that allows the manager to compare the sales performance of different service sites and to determine how total sales compare with those projected in the budget.

There are many other types of financial reports that you may find useful. Cost and revenue information can be used by managers at many different levels to assess program performance and examine the results of any changes in program procedures, structure, or design. The system can provide such information as the cost of resource used, the cost of providing each type of service to clients, and the amount of money generated by the different types of services.

9

Managing Safety and Security

Security is the condition of being protected against danger or loss. In the general sense, security is a concept similar to safety. The nuance between the two is an added emphasis on being protected from dangers that originate from outside. Individuals or actions that encroach upon the condition of protection are responsible for the breach of security. The word "security" in general usage is synonymous with "safety," but as a technical term "security" means that something not only is secure but that it has been secured.

Security has to be compared and contrasted with other related concepts: Safety, continuity, reliability. The key difference between security and reliability is that security must take into account the actions of active malicious agents attempting to cause destruction. It is very often true that people's perception of security is not directly related to actual security.

Hotel companies that do make the decision to "go global," as well as those already operating offshore, will benefit from addressing a key area of business risk-physical security and other life safety risks arising from various forms of workplace violence and other crime. International expansion mergers, deregulation and privatisation often drive revenue growth, operational efficiencies and benefits to customers. But they can also be breeders of employee discontent, labour unrest, potential criminal disruption and terrorist actions. Fire safety is also a major area of risk and source of litigation for organisations around the world. Because of these risks, hospitality organisations doing business in foreign markets should avoid the mistake of replicating the management models, construction design, security systems and training programmes that work for them in their home countries. Just as risk must be carefully assessed in the marketing and financial arenas, hospitality companies also need rigorous risk "audits" when it comes to life safety systems and crisis management.

HOTEL SECURITY PROBLEMS

Security aspect of systems in hotel is equally important to physical and persons' security.

— Record all losses and missing items immediately.

— Inventory control should be proper.

— Auditing should be done on regular basis.

— Proper system for cash receipts and disbursements should be made.

The term 'systems' mean the operations of the hotel e.g. all the equipment used for operation, procedures laid down for operations and policies to be followed. The objective of such security is to safeguard the assets of the hotel. Systems, procedures and the policies followed properly shall safeguard the assets and shall increase the life span of equipment as well as avoid any breakdown maintenance. This would mean the following:

— *Fix duties and assign responsibility*: Fix duties of the staff so that people do their duties and don't interfere with others' work. This will help in pinpointing responsibility in case of theft, losses due to negligence and any other similar eventuality. Make people responsible for what they are doing and for equipment they are handling.

— Make surprise checks.

— Bonding of employees: People who have access to liquid assets should be bonded so that in case of any theft etc. the concerned person may be caught.

— Hiring of an independent agency for checking of your systems of security.

The most common security problems are in guest rooms. Next comes the parking area. By using the electronic card key system we can reduce Room Break-Ins cases. Sometime even the traditional cards keys themselves are easy to copy. It is important to keep pace with technology and the management should have foresight while choosing a system that is compatible with future trends of technology or enhancement. Appoint a systems manager to provide the 'band aid' support to your systems. The supervision staff would be trained to change their supervisory techniques and vision. Proper training to staff should be given before installing the system. The hotel can reduce electricity consumption through the key card operated energy saving system, which could distinguish between a guest and a maid.

Set up security nets with bags and body searches for guests who are not known to the staff. Banqueting suites should be security checked and locked after use; it way all nonpublic areas should be treated. All cluttered items should be removed as they interfere in security checks. Freestanding deep ashtrays are suspicious objects. Toilets should be checked. Staff entrances should be secured at night. Goods received and bags should be checked and kept tidy. If we get a scare or an alert we should not ask people to evacuate the building as we could be sending them into a danger area. Warn them to stay away from windows and leave them slightly open. Heavy curtains should be closed. If a bomb threat is received the telephonist must note carefully what exactly is said, what time the call is received, the sex, and accent of the caller and background noise if any. After the alert the G.M. should stay put in lobby where he can be reached immediately. The duties and responsibilities of staff during such emergencies should be defined. Work closely with police to keep updated on sensitive events in the area.

Bring in sniffer dogs before a big conference commences. Chambermaids and housekeeper should be trained to keep security checks in room; particularly if they notice that the carpet has been moved, they must report immediately. Just asking a guest "Can I help you?" makes people aware that we are vigilant. Fire officers should be called in weekly to check firefighting system. A drill in fire fighting and first aid should be given to all staff members. Practice in building evacuation is done twice a year.

The housekeeping workers can do a great deal to minimise the risk of accidents. The genuine accident is really very rare; most result from oversight or carelessness. It will never be possible to eliminate accidents completely but if the receptionist takes accident prevention seriously and is aware of the possible hazards then she may help to make her organisation a safer place to work. Frayed carpets, torn or badly worn linoleum, projecting nails, loose floorboards and highly polished floors—all bring about falls. Any danger spots such as these should be noted by the receptionist and reported to the management. Visitors are always unaware of potential hazards such as an unexpected step up or down, swing doors that fly open violently and steep stairs. When a lift is installed in the building visitors should always violently and steep stairs. When a lift is installed in the building visitors always is escorted to the required floor by a messenger or by the receptionist herself.

Deliveries of stationery and office requisites should not be left lying around the reception area to trap the visitor. These should be stacked neatly out of the way until a messenger or porter arrives to remove them. The porter or messenger should not be allowed to carry awkward or extremely heavy parcels as this in itself may bring about an accident. The receptionist should always use a safe stepladder to reach high shelves. Heavy books, box files and ledgers that are balanced precariously on a shelf may fall at the slightest vibration so they need to be stored very securely. When filing cabinets are overloaded in the top drawers, or when more than one drawer is opened at a time, they may topple forward with very nasty consequences.

A great many mishaps are caused by 'bumping' into someone. Personnel become absorbed in a report or some important papers while walking across the reception area. They may push open glass doors without looking to see if someone is on the other side and person struck by a glass door could suffer serious facial injuries. There is not really very much a receptionist can do here except to draw attention to such a situation by displaying a warning notice or special warning posters. The staff should provide plenty of ashtrays and pleasantly request all visitors to use them if they smoke. cigarettes left smouldering on the edges of tables or window - sills are a fire hazard. The staff should not empty ash trays into a waste paper basket without ensuring that all cigarettes are thoroughly extinguished and wastepaper baskets should not be placed too near to an electric fire or other heating appliance. All personnel should know fire precautions.

The housekeeping staff should be aware of the positions of all the fire extinguishers an should know the drill for evacuating the premises in case of fire. The staff must also know how to prevent the rapid spread of the fire by closing windows and doors and unplugging all the electrical appliances. He should, personally, escort visitors to safety if possible. In a hotel, however, it would not be possible for the receptionist to make himself responsible for the visitors. The current fire precautions, however, ensure that fire escapes are provided and fire doors installed. Electrical cables, switches and plugs must be carefully maintained and not left to fall into disrepair. Plugs must be earthed and no sockets should be overloaded, electric machines such as duplicators should have a 'fail-safe' switch and electric fires must be guarded. The Socket should be switched off and the plug removed when equipment is not in use.

The housekeeping staff may contribute tremendously to make the organisation to safer place to work by own vigilance and by warning the management of potential danger spots. It is the duty of the employer to consult representatives of the employees with a view to enable him and his employees to co-operate effectively in promoting and developing the health and safety at work of the employees and in making sure that the measures are effective. It is the housekeeping employer's duty to provide and maintain a safe environment in which employees may work. It is the duty of the employees to take reasonable safety precautions and to co-operate with the management in making the organisation's premises a safer and healthier place to work.

Threats to Privacy

It is the duty of housekeeping staff to protect the privacy of its guests-even and perhaps especially if they are in the public eye. It is very tempting to tell one's friends all about a well-know person who might be staying at your hotel, but you will have no control over the information passed over from your friends to their own friends. In no time at all, your guest may be pestered by fans, autograph hunters, paparazzi and reporters. However, it is not only the privacy of well-known guests that must be respected. Every one of our guests is entitled to his or her own privacy and steps must be taken to ensure that information about our guests is not divulged to outsiders.

Giving room numbers to individuals other than the persons being accommodated in those rooms is unethical and should be avoided at all costs. There is a tendency amongst representatives locally to divulge room numbers to taxi drivers, restaurants etc. It may prove difficult to ascertain whether the breach of confidentiality is the responsibility of the hotel or not, but guests have every right to hold the hotelier accountable.

Threats to Property

The hotelier's liability is limited, it is in the interests of the hotel to ensure the safety of its guests and their property - if anything to protect the reputation of the hotel. If the hotel is in an unsafe area, or in an area roamed by unscrupulous characters, guests should be made aware of this -especially if they intend to venture out of the hotel at night. In India, hotels should be especially aware of the problems caused by prostitution. Prostitution is not per se illegal but a hotel would be acting illegally if it were to knowingly encourage or allow prostitution within its premises. It is not for us to make a general characterisation of prostitutes, but some prostitutes may well be thieves and since hotel guests will often negate their involvement with a prostitute they may accuse hotel staff of pilfering their property rather than admit to the fact that they hosted a girl in their room. Unfortunately, we must also face the fact that there are instances where guests are robbed by staff. There may be a "social divide" between staff and guests, which may lead the former to pilfer money or valuable items from a guest. If the hotel has a policy of randomly checking staff's property before they leave the hotel, this may act as a deterrent and waive the hotel's liability should this arise.

Confidence tricksters or conmen may also find themselves into a hotel. There is very little a hotel can do if a confidence trickster makes his way into a guest's "life". These type of people often settle their own room accounts and are simply guests from a hotel point of view. However, when the identity of a conman is known the hotel is ethically bound to blacklist him and refuse him accommodation in the hotel. Guests themselves may also threaten each other's enjoyment. If a traveller turns up in a drunken state asking for a room a hotel is entitled to refuse him on the grounds that he is not a fit state to be received. This is true even if he already has a booking, as he has broken one of the implied conditions of the contract. Similarly if the guest misbehaves throughout his stay the hotel is not obliged to let him stay. When guests complain about being kept awake by a noisy couple or a drunkard next door, it is not good enough to tell a guest that "nothing can be done about that." One must employ considerable tact in dealing with such situations.

Personal Care Services

Good personal service is about creating a sense of well being in our customers-a feeling that their needs are being met, that their business is valued, that they matter to us. It is difficult to define the personal service concept as it cannot be weighed or measured. Good service will mean different things to different people and the challenge for people working in the hotel and tourism industry is to anticipate and meet as far as possible the needs of all our customers. There are two main types of service - material and personal. The term "material service" relates to the quality, quantity, price and timing of food, drink, physical comfort, information and working methods. Material service is generally something concrete and visible that the customer can easily identify. It would not be possible to provide good personal service without the back up of good material service. Yet often the customer is unmoved by the material service no matter how good a standard it is, and it often has, at best, only a neutral effect on him. Customers are more likely to comment on material service when it is below standard than to praise it.

Because material service is easier to define and analyse, most companies give priority to this in terms of investment and advertising aspects of their business. Yet research shows that it is the level of personal service that is most often the deciding factor in customers' choice and that where the material service falls below par, it may well be forgiven if the customer is treated with warmth and kindness. Personal service is about creating a sense of well being in our customers—making them feel welcome and valued while at the same time ensuring that their needs are looked after.

Personal service is not tangible therefore it is difficult to measure, as it is largely more emotional that rational and is very subjective. While you may not be able to actually see personal service, you will notice if it is not there. The key to success in the hotel business is to provide a high standard of both material and personal service - every hotel supplies its guests with food, drink and accommodation but if your hotel is also providing a high level of personal service then you will have the competitive edge. That is the reason you and the job you do are so important to the business - you are the key -to providing a high level of personal service.

There are three parties involved in customer care and they are: (a) the customer, (b) the company and (c) you. All three parties can feel the benefits of good and effective customer care—there is something in it for everyone and not just the customer. These benefits may be identified as follows:

— For the Customer
— pleasant experience
— attractive, welcoming surroundings
— helpful, interested staff
— finding what they want
— being cared for and treated as an individual
— respect and recognition

For the Company

— satisfied customers
— customer loyalty and goodwill
— increased sales and profit
— good "word of mouth" publicity
— staying ahead of the competition
— meeting customers' needs for better service
— repeat business as satisfied customers will return again and again
— greater job satisfaction for staff

For You

— customers being pleasant to you
— the pleasure of seeing the customer satisfied
— the satisfaction of doing a good job and using your skills and knowledge
— knowing you have done your best
— the satisfaction of being pleasant to people and giving them what they want
— more happiness, less stress

Don't confuse the idea of offering a perfect service with the idea of having the perfect product. It is possible to deliver a really good service to guests in a hotel or guest house that has no star rating and it is also possible to deliver a poor quality service in a five star hotel! You are the central and key element in the delivery of quality - you are in the driving seat—you have a very important role to play.

Working in the hotel business means coming in contact with a wide cross-section of the public. In your job you will have to learn to recognise. Who your different types of customers are and the service that they will both expect and require - meeting their different needs to the highest possible standard is customer-care in action. Some of the obvious ones are:

— *The business and conference customers*: They will expect and demand an efficient professional service to act as a backup to their activities. Their priorities might be punctuality, availability of high standard secretarial services, privacy and unobtrusive service.

— *The holidaymaker or tourist*: They may be more interested in the hotels leisure facilities, friendly service and value for money.

It is your job to identify these individual needs and to ensure the service you provide matches if not exceeds the guest's expectations. The less obvious type of customer is those who may have special needs, requiring understanding and sensitive handling, such as:

— *The elderly*. Older customers may have mobility problems and may tire easily. Some people in their eighties are very active, others are not. Your common sense should tell you if they need special help. Elderly visitors should be treated with respect and patience.

— *Children*.Families comprise a major segment of the holiday market, yet many staff appear to tolerate children under sufferance. Parents and children will appreciate staff who facilitate and welcome families.

— *Disabled visitors.* Disabled visitors can easily be handicapped not by their disability but by staff attitudes towards them. Try to treat them as you would any other visitor, while making allowances for their disability. Guests with restricted hearing may not be able to benefit from your announcements. During a conversation, they may be trying to lip read so it is important that you face them and speak very clearly. If necessary write down the information for that you face them and speak very clearly. If necessary write down the information for them. Similarly blind or partially sighted people may require special assistance.

— *Overseas visitors.* It helps to understand and respect some of the basic cultural differences between various nationalities so as to avoid offending visitors unwillingly. For instance, recognising religious dietary restrictions and codes of behaviour will help you in your understanding of guests needs. Caring, being professionally concerned and noticing things is one of the secrets of success in the hospitality industry. If you care about others, you take trouble to see that they are comfortable and have everything they need. Caring is both the way you do things and the reason why you do them.

Handling Complaints

People staying in a hotel would have high expectations of everything going well. When something does go wrong, they will often confront the first staff member they can find. The complaint will often be unrelated to you personally or to your job, but they will still expect you to solve the problem. Knowing how to respond to a complaint and how to resolve the problem will be of great importance to you in your job as a receptionist. In many ways you should consider a genuine complaint as an opportunity and turn it around to your advantage.

Remember, customers don't always complain when they have reason to. Unspoken dissatisfaction is the most damaging to any business, whereas a complaint allows you the opportunity to remedy the situation and to regain the customer's goodwill.

Most complaints are genuine and should be regarded as a very important source of information about the quality of your service or product. While many complaints are received in hotels about efficiency and the product itself, a high proportion concern staff and the way they treat customers. Therefore proper handling of a complaint can make a very favorable impression.

Feelings of anger and upset can cause customers to react differently as they complain. Some appear aggressive and loud, others are timid and there are others who calmly insist on their rights. Staffs have to cope with the moods as well as the facts of the complaint. Showing empathy - that you appreciate how the customer feels - will make things easier. It is important to avoid arguing with customers who complain - they are already angry and upset.

It is important to avoid justifying or making excuses from your own or the company's viewpoint - customers are not interested in excuses, they want results. While all complaints are different and will need a different approach, the following listen techniques in six steps offers a guideline for dealing with them.

1. *Lend an ear to the customer's problems*: The first thing he wants to do is get it off his chest. Pay concerned attention to his story. If he is really angry, let him blow his top. Avoid interrupting and never show annoyance, resentment or fear.
2. *Identify the important points*: While you are listening, sort out the important facts of the situation. Keep an open mind. If necessary, ask clarifying questions,

without appearing to crossexamine the customer or doubt his judgment.

3. *Sympathise*: "I'm sorry", is the least that can be said in the circumstances. Show that you are concerned and regret the problem or the inconvenience caused. But don't keep on apologising or be too willing to admit your hotel is at fault.
4. *Thank the customer*: Thank the customer for bringing the matter to your attention and show that the trouble he is taking in making the complaint is appreciated by you.
5. *Explain what can be done*: Make sure the customer understands what you and the company can and will do about the complaint.
6. *Now act quickly*: Whatever is to be done by yourself or anyone else, ensure that it is done quickly and efficiently.

Always try and put yourself in the customer's shoes when dealing with a complaint. Ask yourself how you would like to be treated in the same circumstances. All customers are important, no matter what the reason is that makes them demanding. You will find that most customers are reasonable - however you need to be able to deal with the unreasonable. Turn the difficult customer's strength against them. The following tips may help to you, should you find yourself faced with a "difficult" customer:

Type	Technique
Argumentative	Do not argue back
Disbelieving	Keep to the facts, not opinions
Expert	Give the facts and let the customer express his views
Indecisive	Show range of alternatives

Nervous	Establish confidence, do not rush
Pompous	Allow customers to maintain dignity
Short-tempered	Tact, patience and firm response
Silent	Use questioning technique

You should know the policy and procedures in your hotel for both handling and reporting complaints. If you remember, complaints should be regarded as an opportunity - not just an opportunity to make amends to the guest but also to get to the source of the problem to ensure it does not happen again. It is therefore essential that the relevant information is filtered back to the appropriate person or department so as the hotel can safeguard against the same problem occurring again and again. You should record all complaints according to the hotel policy and make sure your supervisor knows about it. The best way to deal with a complaint is to prevent it from occurring.

Both compliments and complaints are a comment from customers on the service, which they have received and are also an opportunity, to improve service. Compliments, which are passed on to staff, are a useful means of increasing motivation and of raising standards throughout the business. Praise for a job well done is always very satisfying so accept compliments from customers graciously and be sure that they are passed on to staff members concerned and that your manager or supervisor is made aware of the positive feedback. Keeping a record of special compliments and displaying thank-you letters and complimentary guest comment cards can give staff a welcome morale boost.

Problem solving calls for systematic handling and application of innate and acquired skills. There are four basic steps to handle such problematic situations:

— Listen to the problem.
— Understand the problem.
— Find solutions to the problem.
— Follow-up on the solution.

On analysing these four steps, one realises the need for all the security personnel, to be able to listen, empathize and reason. This is because, it is their responsibility to deal with and solve difficult problems. It is important, that they don't view problem solving as a problem in itself. All security personnel should have stress and event management skills so that they are able to solve problems effectively.

The first step of problem solving, i.e. listening, should be a spontaneous reaction. This skill, if not inherently present should be cultivated. Listening is essential to understand the gravity of the problem a guest is facing. It leads to better analysis and quick resolution. Following are the guidelines that can help in honing the listening skills: One should be very attentive while listening to the guest. This can be achieved by maintaining constant eye contact and making a note of the complaints made by the guest. It is very important that one doesn't continue or conduct any activity which might convey that the personnel is distracted or is not interested. While a conversation is going on, especially when the guest is complaining, wait for your turn to speak. Do not interrupt a guest when he is talking to you. Let him finish explaining his problem first.

Accept the complaint in a positive manner, do not react in anger to a guest who is already in a complaining mood. Anger is a negative emotion and must be avoided as it is known to restrict listening and the assimilation of the conversation. It is important to take the onus of the problem. Apologize for the existing situation the guest is in and assure him of corrective measures. Under no circumstances should you evade solving a problem, by shifting the onus to someone else or passing the buck. This may only lead to an argument, which is a clear indication of the inefficiency of the security personnel in handling the guest and the problem.

Secondly, does it matter who created the problem? Desist from ducking the problem or acting as if it is a normal occurrence and hence not a problem at all. Refrain from blaming colleagues or seniors for the problem. Shifting blame reflects poorly on the organisation. One should understand that good communication always comes from good listening. Good listening reflects sincerity and concern for the guest. Sincerity in tone strengthens his belief in your ability to solve his problem. At any given time convey positive body language. This affirms your sincerity and earnestness in solving the problem and this, in turn, converts a guests' negative attitude towards your organisation, into a positive one.

The second step to problem solving is to understand the problem. This is done by defining the problem on hand. What is a problem? A problem is a situation, which occurs when the actual state of affairs differs from the desired state of affairs. For example, a guest staying with the property desires absolute safety and security standards being adopted by the hotel, for himself and his belongings. It may so happen that he complains about his laptop being stolen from the seminar he was attending at the banquet hall. Now, that is a problem and it arises only when a guest is in a situation wherein he feels threatened, or when he is faced with an event that may cause damage or loss to his person or his belongings. Unless otherwise necessitated, most problems are never referred to local law enforcing authorities. The reason could be personal and varied from the guest's point of view.

When the problem is grievous, like a guest found dead in the room or smuggled goods, drugs in the room, in such cases the management is known to consent to reference of the matter, to the police. Even in such situations, the security personnel cannot be absolved of the lack in their initial spadework. As 'circumstances cannot lie, witnesses can and do', hence it is very important to visit the scene of the problem, example, if a guest is found dead in his room, a visit and check of his room could help determine the consequences and motive of the incident and one can establish the cause, that is, whether the cause of the death is natural or unnatural. If it is an unnatural death, the cause can be further narrowed down. Every security officer should be able to determine what physical clues at the scene of the problem will provide him with scientific evidence. It should be remembered that most physical evidence becomes useless if inefficiently handled.

Integrated Security System

A lodging property's management must evaluate whether a special security presence is warranted by its property's security requirements. If it is, management must decide how that presence may best be integrated with the operation of the hotel. A management team's commitment to the concept of security as a vital function within its hotel is necessary to integrate security into the day-to-day operation and administration of the property.

Setting up such as integrated security system is a process that involves many elements. These may include establishing working relationships with local law enforcement agencies, choosing whether to use in-house or contract security personnel, and creating an appropriate and effective security training programme for all personnel. Because the communities in which they are located affect hotels, a property's management may gain insight into potential security problems by looking at the crime rate and past experiences of the property and surrounding community. Liaisons with police authorities and neighboring lodging properties can help management gain an understanding of the nature and extent of local crime problems. Review with local law enforcement agencies the crime experience, trends, and current problems of your property's locale. Developing such liaisons often results in clear benefits. In some residential communities, local organisations have developed community crime watch programmes in their areas; such programmes attempt to remote neighborhood or block activities to develop an awareness of suspicious persons or actions. Some lodging properties have adopted a similar concept that involves developing a telephone network that notifies both police and participating lodging properties when a crime has happened. Each property notified, in turn, may call other properties in the network. Some properties find that such a programme may aid the security efforts of the participating lodging establishments. However, such a programme should be cleared with local counsel to ensure that the information disseminated does not violate Federal Trade commission regulations or other federal or local laws, or result in a suit for defamation or libel. Public safety is, of course, the specific responsibility of law enforcement agencies.

In conjunction with a property's security programme, its management should cultivate cooperative liaison with the local b ranch of these agencies. Inform them of your concern and interest in the security of your property, your guests, and ad your employees. Invite the appropriate law enforcement personnel to visit your property so they can become familiar with it. Some hotels hire off - duty police personnel as additional security staff on special occasions. If possible, review security procedures with the local authorities. Be sure to request police guidance in crime prevention and always document such efforts. A good relationship with local law enforcement agencies can often encourage a prompt response to security incidents and will probable result in your property benefiting from more frequent police patrols. Police presence can also be a deterrent to certain crimes; measurable reductions in total crimes have been noted in some cases in which liaison relationships have been developed. Good relationships may also be very helpful and much appreciated following a security incident or during an emergency. Frequently, community police budget limitations within a jurisdiction do not permit an evaluation of crime as it relates to a specific hotel. Where a crime unit does exist within a law enforcement agency, a full review of community and lodging industry crime experience may be available.

Unfortunately, law enforcement agencies and private security personnel have not always cooperated well with each other. Police have sometimes viewed private security efforts as staffed with poorly trained older (or retired) personnel who are largely ineffective and even fairly apathetic. In today's changing security scene, this stereotype often does an injustice to a lodging property's security personnel as private security has become more professional and sophisticated. Better communication is the key to educating local law enforcement agencies about the broad scope of a lodging property's security programme and about the growing professionalism of the industry's security personnel.

The most effective cooperation results when both the police and the property understand the needs of the other. The police should know enough about a property and its security programme to be able to offer appropriate assistance in a given situation. They should be informed of any special events or visitors that may involve an unusual security risk at the property. On the other hand, the property' staff should have a basic understanding of police procedures so that they can be of greatest assistance to the police once they arrive.

Local law enforcement authorities will be able to explain the type of assistance they would find most helpful. This information should be included in a property's ongoing security training programme. In one positive development, some police departments have gone so far as to assign a number of detectives to work directly with hotel security directors. These detectives can teach a property's personnel about police procedures and needs, offer guidance to the staff about what to watch for, and share information about any crime patterns in the area that may affect the property. At the same time, they learn about the property and its security system, improving the likelihood of effective police response in times of need.

A hotel must choose whether to hire staff as full-time personnel, to contract with a local security company, to arrange for part-time protection with local off-duty police personnel, or to use any combination of these or other options. Because of a facility's size and organisational structure, it may be appropriate to assign security responsibility to a member of the management staff, such as a resident or assistant manager, a chief engineer, or the human resources director. Larger hotels have full-time security staffs, with one or more employees on each shift.

Smaller properties may not be able to afford a full-time hotel employees may be an appropriate approach. If management decides the property needs a security department, it must determine whether the department should be a proprietary unit with in - house staff functions or a security programme run through a reputable, licensed contract security company. In some situations, it may be feasible to employ off-duty police to cover certain hours of operation while e property's staff provides daytime coverage as one of their responsibilities. If the security department or function is integrated into the property, additional considerations include determining whether the staff will wear uniforms, whether certain or all members of the security staff will be armed, and whether there are shifts on which security personnel need not be assigned. All decisions concerning security deserve careful thought and should be discussed with legal counsel. Each option has its adherents.

The proponents of contract security organisations argue that such organisations can provide sophisticated services at considerable savings. In addition, they assert that a reputable contract Security Company will provide thoroughly screened, tested, and trained personnel. It may also provide consulting services, including in-depth surveys of hotel security requirements, electronic audio countermeasure sweeps (a debugging tactic), data processing security, and assistance in contingency planning for bomb threats and natural disasters. Finally, they contend that an in-house security staff may become too familiar and friendly with the other employees.

If a guard catches a friend stealing, he or she might hesitate to report that friend. Some people believe that this situation may be less likely to occur if the security personnel are supplied by an n outside agency. In selecting a security company, make sure that extensive guard training geared specifically to each facility, is provided. Review contract and insurance requirements (i.e., named insured clauses and requirements for proof of insurance) with legal counsel. Check the previous lodging experience of the company management and line security staff, as well as specific training in dealing with guests, employees and others. If your state or community requires such agencies to be certified, verify that the agency you choose meets this legal requirement. Be clear and specific regarding the services to be provided by the contract organisation. Require the security firm to conduct frequent unannounced inspections, day and night, by supervisory personnel to ensure that its guards re in compliance with company regulations. Determine whether the security service can provide a sufficient number of personnel on short notice in the case of a large-scale emergency. Insist that security officers be required to file daily and unusual incident reports.

Determine the percentage of the security firm's hotel customers retained on an annual basis; rates of retention are an excellent indication of a company's service level. When hotel management gives orders or instructions to the contract employee, a different relationship is established. The responsibility for the actions of the contract security office becomes blurred, and there are instances in which the contract employee has been considered as a workers' compensation case for the property rather than for the contract security company.

Contract companies have held and prevailed that the instructions from the hotel executive may have placed the contract employee in jeopardy and may have been contributory to workers' compensation incident. In other instances, the contract employee has turned to his or her company for the workers' compensation only. A contract security organisation will almost always be willing to perform an indepth security survey for a property if the property has not already performed one for itself or had one performed by another agency.

Proponents of proprietary or in-house security departments point out a number of advantages to this system. They emphasize the fact that the hotel has greater control over security officers or staff members without intermediate outside supervision. They also argue that training for in-house security staff members can be much more directly related to the lodging industry. They believe that those within the industry than more effectively address the peculiarities and special needs of the industry by those in a contractual relationship with the industry. In addition, they emphasize that the quality of personnel is under the direct control of the hotel in a proprietary system, rather than under the control of the contract security company, and that the director and staff of an in-house department are more effectively integrated with the other departments and personnel of the property. If the security staff is in-house, then the security director can be a member of the property's executive committee, an action that would not be possible with a contract staff and supervision. They point out that a greater sense of loyalty may be developed among an in-house staff since career paths can be established that move security personnel into other roles in the organisation. Finally, another important concern is the constant turnover of contract security employees.

Some properties use off-duty police officers for their security staff. There are certain benefits associated with this practice. Such officers have superior training in reacting to and dealing with crimes and other emergencies, they understand the law, they are used to dealing with people, they may be better able to identify known criminals, they are immediately recognised as authorities, and they often do in fact have more authority than ordinary citizens. In addition, police liaison and response may be enhanced. However, there may be potential drawbacks as well. First, police officers may be oriented more toward apprehension functions than toward prevention. Second, some jurisdictions require off-duty officers to be armed and this may not be desirable. In addition, off-duty officers may not be permitted to wear uniforms in some jurisdictions. Finally, an officer may be working at the hotel following a full-duty police shift and may be fatigued.

Security concerns should be addressed during the selection and hiring of all employees. It is especially important, though, when hiring a member of the security department, given that this individual is responsible for the protection of persons and assets on the property. If legal counsel approves, the hotel could use and an authorisation statement and affidavit. Such a statement, signed by the job applicant, allows the property to more easily investigate the applicant's background. Bonding (insuring for protection from employee theft) through an insurance company permits more effective screening of applicants and is certainly warranted in the case of security staff members who, by virtue of their function, have access to most areas of the hotel. It is appropriate to have everyone employed as a vehicle driver to have a police background check for traffic violations. This background check should be done before hiring and at least annually from that time on. This procedure applies not only to specialised employees, such as airport buss drivers, but for other employees who may drive a hotel vehicle as part of their other assigned duties, such as a maintenance staff member. Properties must also decide how they will schedule security staff on the property.

Disaster Management

Keeping your premises safe can save lives. It can also help in defending against allegations of negligence should a disaster occur. Consider the lesson of the hotel that let dust and linen accumulate in linen chutes: when the accumulation caused an otherwise containable fire to spread and cause substantial damage, they were held liable.

During an emergency, you must be able to alert your guests, deploy personnel, and summon emergency services quickly. For example, checking to see how bad a fire is before calling the fire department may make fighting the fire more difficult and subject the hotel to liability. The evacuation guides on the back of hotel room doors do not constitute an "emergency plan." Your plan should ensure that guests receive adequate warning of an emergency and provide for their effective evacuation. Your plan should provide for ongoing education to employees and for conducting periodic drills to ensure compliance with the plan. Hotels may be held liable for losses caused by a disaster if they don't have a plan, if the plan is inadequate, or if they fail to follow the plan.

When disaster strikes:

— *Warn guests of the emergency*: You have a duty to warn guests of an emergency: do not delay! Hotels can be held liable for a failure to warn guests of an emergency or for an unduly delayed warning. You may not have to physically accompany guests out of the hotel, but you can be held liable if blocked exists or inadequate lighting in halls and stairwells impedes evacuation.

— *Call for medical assistance:* Hotels have a legal obligation to call for medical assistance when a guest is seriously ill or suffers serious injury. Unnecessary delays in summoning emergency help can subject the hotel to liability. Also keep in mind the hotel that provided a physician's assistant to treat guests was held liable when the assistant prescribed the wrong medicine resulting in the death of the guest: be wary of providing your own medical care.

If your hotel is safe, don't raise the rates. If your hotel survives a disaster and other hotels in the vicinity do not survive, the market value of your safe hotel rooms will skyrocket. However, think twice before raising your rates. Hotels may be held liable for price gouging under state law and be ordered to refund the costs of rooms to customers. Hotels may also be held liable for deceptive business practices. If your hotel is no longer able to house and provide services to guests after a disaster, it is unlikely you have a legal obligation to find your guests other housing. Of course, in the interest of customer relations and goodwill, providing as much service as possible is the wisest course for those in the hospitality industry.

Bibliography

Abel, Dorothy Lois. *Making housekeeping easy.* New York: Funk and Wagnalls, 1948.

Abell, L. G. *The skillful housewife's book: or, Complete guide to domestic cookery, taste, comfort and economy. Embracing 659 receipts, pertaining to household duties, the care of health, gardening, flowers, birds, education of children etc., etc.* New York: A. O. Moore, 1852.

Adams, Agatha Boyd. *The homemaker enlists.* Chapel Hill N.C.: the University of North Carolina Press, 1943.

Babcock, Emma Whitcomb. *Household hints.* New York: D. Appleton and company, 1881.

Balderston, Lydia Ray. *Housekeeping workbook how to do it—house care and cleaning.* Chicago, Philadelphia: J. B. Lippincott company, 1935.

Baxter, Lucia Allen Millet. *Housekeepers handy book.* Boston and New York: Houghton Mifflin company, 1913.

Beecher, Henry Ward. *All around the house, or, How to make homes happy.* New York: D. Appleton and Co., 1881.

Black. *Hints to young housekeepers.* London: W. Collins, 1880.

Black, Clementina. *A new way of housekeeping.* London etc.: W. Collins Sons & Co. Ltd., 1918.

Campbell, Helen. *The easiest way in housekeeping and cooking.* Boston: Roberts bros., 1903.

Creamer, Jack B. *The handy household manual.* Chicago: Ziff-Davis Pub. Co., 1945.

De Both, Jessie Marie. *Modern household encyclopedia.* Chicago: J. G. Ferguson, 1948.

Frederick, Christine. *The ignoramus book of housekeeping*. New York: Sears Pub. Co. inc., 1932.

Gilman, Charlotte Perkins. *The home, its work and influence.* New York: McClure Phillips & co., 1910.

Hale, Sarah Josepha Buell. *Manners; happy homes and good society all the year round.* Boston: Lee and Shepard, 1889.

Harland, Marion. *The housekeeper's week.* Indianapolis: The Bobbs-Merrill company, 1908.

Herndon, James B. and Herndon/Vehling Collection. *The Domestic service guide: to housekeeping, practical cookery.* London: Lockwood, 1865.

Hoover Company. *House cleaning and home management manual.* North Canton, 1950.

Hopkins, Mary Alden. *Profits from courtesy: handbook of business etiquette.* Melrose Mass: Educational Service Bureau, 1937.

James, Alice L. *Housekeeping for two; a practical guide for beginners.* New York London: G.P. Putnam's sons, 1909.

Kirkland, E. S. *Dora's housekeeping.* Chicago: A.C. McClurg & company, 1899.

Prince, Jane. *Letters to a young housekeeper.* Boston: House Beautiful Publishing, 1918.

Shepperd, Juniata L. *Handbook of household science.* St. Paul Minn.: Printed by Webb Pub. Co., 1902.

Taylor, Marie Hansen. *Letters to a young housekeeper.* New York: C. Scribner's sons, 1893.

White, Sallie Joy. *Housekeepers and home-makers.* Boston: Jordan Marsh & Co., 1888.

Index

Notes

Notes

Notes

Notes